APPROACHES IN
LINGUISTIC
METHODOLOGY

Edited by

IRMENGARD RAUCH

and

CHARLES T. SCOTT

THE UNIVERSITY OF WISCONSIN PRESS
Madison, Milwaukee, and London
1967

Published by
THE UNIVERSITY OF WISCONSIN PRESS
Madison, Milwaukee, and London

U.S.A.: Box 1379, Madison, Wisconsin, 53701
U.K.: 26–28 Hallam Street, London, W. 1

Printed in the United States of America
by the Waverly Press, Inc., Baltimore, Maryland

Library of Congress Catalog Card Number 66-22863

APPROACHES IN LINGUISTIC METHODOLOGY

TO MURRAY FOWLER

ἐπεὶ ψάμμος ἀριθμὸν περιπέφευγεν,
καὶ κεῖνος ὅσα χάρματ᾽ ἄλλοις ἔθηκεν,
τίς ἂν φράσαι δύναιτο;

—Pindar, *Olympia II*

The preoccupation of linguistics today might be described as the attempt to develop and to demonstrate the most adequate, valid, and mathematically simple approach to language description. Such an attempt implicitly requires a universal theory of the nature of language, and it is a mark of the maturity achieved by their science that linguists are now willing seriously to consider the possibility of universals in language. Nevertheless, in the course of rapid growth, the emergence of vigorous new theories, the clash of 'schools' clamoring for a hearing, there is a real danger that one essential of science, the empirical basis of investigation, should become obscured. In fact, there appears to be a gradual but increasing erosion of objectivity.

The impetus for this volume is the strong sense of concern felt by the contributors over the decline of objectivity in linguistic description. While receptive to the constructive theorizing of any school, the contributors are wary of the stifling effect which, in the long run, would result from the claim to exclusive generality made by any one methodology.

Though certain requirements are common to every adequate linguistic treatment, their formulation into a statement which is to serve as a general principle calls for extreme caution. Thus, for example, Hjelmslev's 'empirical principle' of analysis is in itself universal, but particular methods of analysis are not. The linguist is not confined to a methodological straitjacket; on the contrary, he is required to choose and apply an approach relevant to his data (L. Hjelmslev, *Prolegomena to a theory of language* 11, 22, F. J. Whitfield, trans.; Madison, 1963).

It is for this reason that the present volume offers a sampling of different methodologies. It is further hoped that a worthwhile by-product of presenting varied approaches will be to impress upon students of linguistics the crucial importance, in linguistic description, of judgments objectively formed and objectively maintained.

The authors of this collection met a November 1, 1964 deadline. Due consideration should be given by the reader to the lapse of time between that date and the date of publication.

When the manuscript was submitted to the Press, the contributors were all members of the Linguistic Circle of Madison. In that capacity they dedicate this volume to their esteemed colleague, Murray Fowler, for many years Chairman of the Department of Linguistics at the University of Wisconsin.

Three of the authors, F. G. Cassidy, John C. Street, and Valdis J. Zeps, were indispensable in helping, beyond their particular contributions, to bring the book to completion. To all concerned with *Approaches in linguistic methodology* the editors extend their sincere gratitude.

I. R.
C. T. S.

November 1966

CONTENTS

APPROACHES IN LINGUISTIC METHODOLOGY

INTRODUCTION

The thirteen papers that constitute this collection of diverse 'approaches in linguistic methodology' fall into two principal subdivisions. Eleven essays comprise a group that illustrates the application of a particular methodological procedure to specific linguistic problems. This group can be further subdivided into eight synchronic studies (Cassidy, Chou, Erickson, Robinson, Seifert, Street, Tukey, Whiteley) and three diachronic studies (Rauch, Scott, Zeps). The remaining essays (Hammer and Joos) form a separate group of two metalinguistic statements, the first concerned with a conceptualization of the predominantly mathematical nature of linguistic description, the second treating the problem of delimiting more completely the proper bounds of linguistic investigation. The relationship of the individual contributions to each other and to the overriding theme of the volume is indicated here.

The historical development of linguistic theory has never been a serene progression of ideas accepted without question or debate. Instead, the history of linguistic science, like that of any other science, has been characterized by clashes and controversies, typically involving polar views of either professional interests or theoretical and methodological concepts. The oppositions, e.g. between 'philologists' and 'structuralists', 'mechanistic' and 'mentalistic' views of language description, the 'deterministic' and 'relativistic' interpretations of language change, and the so-called 'item and process' and 'item and arrangement' schools, attest to the recurrence of controversy in the history of the science of linguistics. Typically, however, whenever new foci of interests or lines of opposition have developed, older controversies have tended to lose some of their sharpness and relevance, though fortunately not without having lent some additional precision and refinement to linguistic theory and practice. But often any positive effect is only realized in trends that attempt to rediscover the past, e.g. the current reconnaissance of the once-defunct Stammbaumtheorie.[1]

Terms like 'transformational', 'generative', 'synthetic', 'dynamic', and 'process' are all among the methodological catchwords in linguistics today. Some of them, like 'process', generally label one pole of a conceptual opposition, while others, like 'transformational' or 'generative', usually designate some configuration of theory and practice. This volume is, in large part, an outgrowth of the new concern over the impact of the most recent focus of theoretical interest on current linguistic practice—a concern that is shared by the authors to more than an incidental degree. The collection, then, is a modest attempt to display some of the unities and diversities of contemporary linguistic methodology as illustrated by the work of the contributors either on specific problems or discussion directed at the problem of linguistic methodology in general.

The clearest imprint on present-day methodology is undoubtedly that of generative grammar, or, at the very least, that of the return of the process statement to the forefront of linguistic theory. This, however, is neither the time nor the place to attempt any sort of balanced survey of these approaches to linguistic description from the point of view of their historical importance, nor even to attempt a prognosis of the direction in which the field of linguistics is moving with respect to current controversies.[2] Linguistic theory is still too close to the 'static-dynamic', 'analytic-synthetic' oppositions for these to be seen clearly in their proper perspective.

Nevertheless, even at the risk of arriving at premature conclusions, some favorable and unfavorable aspects of the impact of generative grammar on linguistic methodology can be considered briefly. One advantage (a dubious one, perhaps, in the thinking of some scholars) has been the stern questioning of so-called neo-Bloomfieldian linguistics, along with such arguments as to whether x is, or is not, a phoneme, whether allophones may overlap, and the like. This pruning may have removed the theoretical underpinnings from a number of obviously useful practices, although in some instances at least, such practices may have been found to be independently defensible, e.g. the concept of immediate constituents (Street). In a more positive sense, the advantages of a generative approach are clearer. A formal grammar constructed along Chomskian lines permits an understanding of what in a certain process is specific and what is general, i.e. simple in an explicit fashion, whereas previously only intuitive and/or arbitrary criteria were available for the evaluation of grammatical statements.

Still, a number of negative developments cannot be overlooked. The most serious, and potentially the most damaging, to the discipline of linguistics is the rise of a new wave of discontent, which frequently manifests itself in a dogmatic rejection of older views. Much like their predecessors in the 1930's, a young generation of linguists has found the labors of the previous generation to be of little or no value, and therefore discardable. It is quite possible that such repeated waves of iconoclasm may ultimately contribute to the overall progress of the discipline, although at times it is difficult to see how. Equally serious has been a noticeable disdain of 'mere facts' and a certain amount of unpardonable inaccuracy that has accompanied some recent examples of generative statement. This is not at all inherent in the generative approach, and one can only hope that, in the future, practice and theory will go hand in hand.

Distinct from the generative orientation, but with clearly identifiable crosscurrents, is the contribution of the electronic computer. In principle the computer, like the ordinary typewriter, is no more than an extension of the scholar. Yet the computer has so accelerated routine operations as to make not only a quantitative but also a qualitative difference in linguistic thinking. Noteworthy here is the phrasing of Halle's simplicity criterion: '... economy should be measured by the number of distinctive features utilized. The fewer features mentioned in a description, the greater its economy.'[3] According to this view, the brain is very much like a computer, at least in the sense that storage space is at a premium. So, for that matter, is processing time, and the two are incommensurable: in the case of an electronic computer, the two are optimized in terms of cost. No such common measure is available for the brain qua computer, and Halle's simplicity criterion measures only storage space and discards processing time altogether. Halle is known to be well aware of this.

Considerations such as the above go far beyond a merely quantitative change in the processing of linguistic data, and the impact of the computer as an ally and as an analogue is surely only in its beginnings (Hammer). Many of the inroads of computer-oriented methodology have come to contemporary linguistics via mechanical translation (MT), which has encountered a striking lack of success in meeting its self-proclaimed and well-subsidized goals.[4] Of far greater value to the linguistic profession have been relatively unsophisticated byproducts of MT and related work, especially in the construction of multipurpose scholarly aids and reference works, such as the concordances for the Dead Sea Scrolls, or the lexicological work envisaged by Cassidy ('A descriptive approach to the lexicon').[5]

Scholarly attention to the description of the lexicon has increased considerably. In a generative approach the shape and content of the lexical component of the grammar is of paramount importance. The lexicon is, after all, a very bulky part of the grammar, and economies within it, far from being of incidental interest, are crucial in obtaining a good level of economy for the grammar as a whole. The concern for setting up single base forms for lexical entities, exhibited in Jakobson's 'Russian conjugation'[6] and a number of other articles inspired by it, is most clearly evidenced by Erickson ('The establishment of a verbal base form for Arabic').

In addition to internal economies, the importance of a well-designed lexicon becomes increasingly clear if one considers that all subsequent morphophonemic rules are directly dependent on the initial phonological shape of the lexical component. The categorizing of 'fully conventionalized' phonological shapes of morphemes in Cassidy's paper (cf. above), while of marginal importance for English, is of major importance to Whiteley's data ('Loanwords in linguistic description: A case study from Tanzania, East Africa'), where the problem of 'established' and 'probationary' loans is especially acute. Further, the multiple orientation of the lexicon—toward the syntax, toward the phonology, toward a semology, and the like—becomes clearly apparent when one compares the work of Joos ('The completion of descriptive linguistics') in which the semological aspects of a grammar are treated, with that of Chou ('The uses of *shr* in Mandarin Chinese') in which the syntactical employment of a morpheme in a number of meanings has been subjected to an analysis in depth, and with the exposition of Robinson ('A preliminary design for an analytic grammar of Sanskrit') on the lexicon from a decoder's point of view.

It is paradoxical that even though the computer has now brought within the realm of possibility the testing of statistico-distributional theories of meaning,[7] recent discussions of meaning have taken on a qualitative and discrete orientation.[8] Perhaps, however, this too can be understood from the standpoint of computer-processing: in order for a meaning to be stored in the computer memory, it has to be quantized, and previous distributional measures have not been amenable to such structuring.

The goals and purposes of grammars have been subject to scrutiny from a practical viewpoint as well, and here likewise considerable sophistication has developed. Matters of presentation, even of editorial policy, are of much greater importance in the shaping of the progress of a scholarly discipline than commonly realized. It is extremely important whether a grammar is an encoding (synthetic) one or a decoding (analytic) one, as Robinson (cf. above) demonstrates in a rare reversal of the traditional approach to Sanskrit. In connection with this, the last decades have seen the maturing of instructional books of the 'Russian for Spanish speakers' variety into more sophisticated forms as 'contrastive grammars' where similarities between two or more linguistic systems are emphasized or a framework is chosen to accentuate the contrast (Seifert).

Syntax, formerly the most neglected area of linguistic description, is presently under vigorous if not assiduous cultivation. Tukey's paper ('A model for French syntactic description'), benefiting from the mutual complementarity of three analyses along different perspectives, presents an underlying pattern for the French phrase, which has strong tagmemic overtones, although the technique as constructed by Pike[9] is not formally utilized. Curiously, the two latest works originating at the University of Wisconsin and bearing on syntax—Tukey's paper on French and Joos's study of the English verb (see endnote 8)—although dissimilar in detail, agree in adopting a framework of choices and implications rather than using the expansion technique of so-called phrase-structure rules.

In the development of linguistic theory and practice today, one thing is manifestly clear: the focus of interest in the current practice of synchronic linguistics has shifted from concern with a one-dimensional, compartmentalized view of language structure (phonetics, phonemics, morphology) to a multidimensional view incorporating syntax, morphophonemics, the lexicon, and semantics. This shift in interest is certainly a revolution; among the casualties of the revolution is discovery procedure, or at least the earlier expectation that such a procedure would be a natural outgrowth of more rigorously defined techniques of linguistic analysis.

No comparable revolution has taken place in historical linguistics; nevertheless, a number of new approaches have been explored in diachronic studies. The present collection contains one attempt to extend a traditional notion, viz. reflex, to permit discussion about 'reflexes of rules' (Zeps). Characteristically, however, most historically oriented investigations concentrate on sound change. The interpretive techniques used in a graphemic-phonemic analysis of historical data for the purpose of establishing the time limits of a sound change as a historical event are illustrated by Scott ('On the dating of NE *ee* and *ea* spellings from ME $\bar{e}$ and $\bar{ę}$'). Describing a phonemic change in all its significant details entails numerous additional categories of identification. One of the more controversial categories, that of cause, is discussed in conjunction with a systematized inventory of consonants as possible sound conditioners, and the suggestion is made that as such they may share features with the equally controversial laryngeals (Rauch).

Although historical studies are hardly in the linguistic limelight today, Andrews and Whatmough perceive 'in Historical and Comparative method ... a stirring which ... will become a very marked trend within a decade or two.'[10]

Establishing the characteristic properties of linguistic description, or a metatheory for such description, virtually entails the construction of a prismatic complex. In this complex, such axes as synthetic-analytic, prescriptive-descriptive, static-dynamic, synchronic-diachronic, and abstract-concrete, may intersect quite arbitrarily so that the shape of the descriptive prism need not be absolutely fixed. *Approaches in linguistic methodology* demonstrates a small but representative variety of prismatic shapes.

NOTES

1   Cf. e.g. F. C. Southworth, 'Family-tree diagrams', *Language* 40.557–65 (1964); another direction of rediscovery is that which uncovers the inherent structuralism of centuries-old grammars, as in R. A. Fowkes, 'The linguistic modernity of Jakob Grimm', *Linguistics* 8.56–61 (1964).

2   B. Malmberg, in *New trends in linguistics* E. Carney, trans. (Stockholm, 1964)

offers a very comprehensive historical survey of modern approaches, schools, and areas of linguistic investigation.

3 M. Halle, 'On the role of simplicity in linguistic descriptions', in *The structure of language and its mathematical aspects*, R. Jakobson, ed. (*Proceedings of symposia in applied mathematics*, vol. 12) 90 (Providence, 1961).

4 Cf. R. See, 'Mechanical translation and related language research', *Science* 8 May 1964, 62, and letters written in response to this article beginning with the 3 July 1964 issue.

5 Cf. also E. B. Atwood, *The regional vocabulary of Texas* (Austin, 1962), for a study in which dialectal material has been successfully dealt with by means of data-processing techniques.

6 R. Jakobson, in *Word* 4.155–67 (1948).

7 Cf. e.g. Z. S. Harris, 'Distributional structure', *Word* 10.146–62 (1954); C. E. Osgood, G. J. Suci, and P. H. Tannenbaum, *The measurement of meaning* (Urbana, 1957).

8 Cf. e.g. J. J. Katz and J. A. Fodor, 'The structure of a semantic theory', *Lg.* 39.170–210 (1963); Joos, *The English verb: Form and meanings* (Madison, 1964). Even more curious is the appearance of the stratificational view of grammar by a linguist with an intimate acquaintance with computers, S. M. Lamb, 'Stratificational linguistics as a basis for mechanical translation', *Proceedings of the US–Japan seminar on mechanical translation* (forthcoming). Such apparent discrepancies should illustrate clearly, if indeed such illustration is necessary, that, while the new techniques which are available can serve as catalysts, they by no means determine the form that theoretical and practical innovations may take.

9 K. L. Pike, 'On tagmemes, neé [sic] grammemes', *International journal of American linguistics* 24.273–8 (1958) and *Language in relation to a unified theory of the structure of human behavior* Part III (Glendale, Calif., 1960).

10 S. Andrews Jr. and J. Whatmough, 'Comparative historical linguistics in America', *Trends in European and American linguistics 1930–1960*, C. Mohrmann, A. Sommerfelt, and J. Whatmough, eds., 81 (Utrecht, 1961).

1

A DESCRIPTIVE APPROACH TO THE LEXICON

Frederic G. Cassidy

A 'lexicon' or a 'dictionary' has been traditionally thought of as a list of the words of any language, giving their meanings and sundry other facts about them. Dictionaries have developed out of glossaries, which were bilingual to begin with, as indeed were the first dictionaries: there were no monolingual English dictionaries before the seventeenth century. Since the raison d'être of the dictionary has always been practical—to put a useful tool into people's hands—it has usually been arranged alphabetically 'for ready reference.' When one seeks to deal, however, not with 'a' lexicon but with 'the' lexicon of a language, the matter changes. Now we are talking in the abstract about the totality of words in a language and it is evident that a word-by-word presentation for ready reference is not the desideratum. What should be revealed is the structure of the lexicon as a whole. The method of presentation proposed here is intended to achieve this.

A synchronic description of the lexicon of a language—English for example—should ideally include at least two types of information: an inventory of the lexical units, simple and combined; and an account of the structural patterns into which they fall. The first would therefore present, as nearly as possible:

1. All existing morphs, free and bound (though absolute exhaustiveness could not be attained, as not all forms are ever recorded);
2. All words (conventional combinations of morphs) not already included;
3. All set phrases (established groups of specific words differing as groups from the simple sum of their components).

Each item of the inventory should be given in its phonemic shape, followed by its conventional graphic representation or representations; it should also be identified in some way (by stating its function, giving a synonym or an equivalent restatement, etc.).

If more than a single dialect was to be covered it would be desirable to include diaphonic variants, but allophones would be unnecessary.

For a diachronic treatment an additional number of features would be needed:

4. The time span (by dating) of each item's existence (though again, this cannot be attained, and for the same reason as in (1) above: incompleteness of the evidence);

5. The time span of every conventional graphic representation of each item;

6. The time span of every distinct semantic division ('sense' or 'meaning') of each item (though the technique of dividing meanings cannot be completely objective; at present, a consensus of native speakers is the best evidence attainable; for records of the past a consensus of scholars in the field would be necessary);

7. The source of each item—how or whence it came into the language (yet it would not be necessary, though admittedly valuable, to carry the etymology farther back than the proximate source, since to do so would take one beyond the bounds of the language being described—in this case, English);

8. Allophonic variants when they can be known, though these are not certainly recoverable from written records.

Lexicographers in the past have not had the means, and hardly the goal, of providing such an ideal description. Their purposes have generally been practical and therefore limited: they have sought to help writers and speakers by recording conventional spellings and pronunciations, indicating grammatical functions ('parts of speech'), and elucidating meanings. Their entry lists have generally been selective according to the intended readership (elementary school pupils, the nonspecialist public, specific professional groups, and so on through a wide range). They have presented entries in conventional orthography rather than phonemically, and their practices in regard to bound morphs and set phrases have varied considerably. Many have omitted etymological and other historical information entirely. Many even recently have been less than scientific in gathering and dealing with the data: opinion and value judgments have often taken the place of accurate description.

Great improvement came to lexicography, of course, with the establishment of scientific language study a century or so ago. Such a dictionary as the *Oxford* (or *New*) *English Dictionary* (1885–1932) for the first time had a really full body of historical data to draw upon. Today, with the further improvements in techniques of collection and classification, the ideal begins to be conceivably attainable. By the use of the electronic computer it would now be possible to calculate the relative frequency of usage of each inventory item, or of classes of items similar in form, function, origin, status—whatever classification was structurally relevant.

The ideal description, however, would not be presented in the usual dictionary form. For one thing, a list of entries in conventional orthography does not classify; the only order it has (the alphabetic) is casual. Hence in effect it disguises the second kind of information desired: the lexical structure. Dictionaries in some languages (e.g. Hindustani) improve on this by sorting the initial letters at least into a phonetically meaningful sequence. The ideal English lexicon would systematize even further by presenting the morphs according to their phonemes in phonetic order— for example, the vowels from high to low and front to back; the consonants by classes, in front to back order, and with related pairs (e.g. voiced and unvoiced) kept together. In a representative classification the vocalic segmental phonemes might be /i ɪ e ɛ æ ə u ʊ o ɔ ɑ/ with diphthongal combinations treated as vowel sequences; the consonantal segmental phonemes might be /b p d t g k v f ð θ z s ž š m n ŋ l r h j w/ with affricates treated as consonant sequences. The list would then systematically present in this order all the existing morphs which utilize these segmental phonemes, beginning with the smallest (monophonemic) and proceeding step by step to the larger combinations.

One effective way to organize and present the evidence would be in the form of a grid, with the consonant sequence along one axis and the vowel sequence along the other. Done in this simplest possible way, such a presentation would show:

1. A slot for each MATHEMATICALLY possible combination of phonemes;
2. The ranges of slots which are UNFILLABLE because of phonotactic limitations; and
3. The slots which are actually FILLED with real morphs and those which are not.

Since we already know the phonotactic rules of English, however, this scheme could be improved upon by suppressing the UNFILLABLE slots and thus presenting only the FILLABLE ones as either now FILLED or UNFILLED. It would then be easy to see by the relative numbers of filled slots the degree to which each type of combination is favored, and this scheme might be further refined by using a frequency-count of morphs to judge the functional load of each type. Since structural pressure certainly works to fill slots in the lexicon much as it does to produce symmetry or realignments in the phonemic and morphemic systems, a grid presentation of morphs would show the places where structural pressure probably has worked or is working.

The method could be usefully extended to diachronic study. The date range could be shown for each morph in its slot, its time of appearance and (if it has gone out of use) of disappearance. Changes in the structure of morph classes and the rise and fall of specific patterns (those which are extended or which lose members and are reduced) would become apparent.

The grid presentation could be extended diatopically, to show thus the areas within which each morph is used (which would in effect constitute a kind of 'word geography', though not a comparative one). Conceivably the diachronic and diatopic presentations might be combined, and further, differing stylistic ranks of morphs might be indicated, the result being what might be called a DIASTATIC presentation.

The simplest mathematical list of phoneme combinations just mentioned would soon prove cumbersome, as the proportion of unfillable slots would increase rapidly with the increasing length of phoneme sequences. Even if phonotactic rules were used to eliminate the unfillable slots, the number of fillable ones would remain very large, and the longer the sequences of phonemes, the more unfilled slots there would be. Nevertheless, in any attempt to achieve a really full list of morphs this method would be found useful because it would ignore no possibilities, would be eminently suited to use of the computer, and would display the results so as to reveal structural relationships within the total lexicon.

Limiting ourselves, for purposes of illustration, to the monosyllabic morph, let us consider how a grid presentation of current English might proceed. (For simplicity's sake we present only the segmental phonemes; in a full description, suprasegmentals would of course also have to be taken into account.) In the following list, V = vowel phoneme; C = consonant phoneme. All V and C may come medially, but:

V that may be initial: /i ɪ e ɛ æ ə u ʊ o ɔ ɑ/   (11)
V that may be final: /i e u o ɔ ɑ/   (6)
C that may be initial: /b p d t g k v f ð θ z s š m n l r h j w/   (20)
C that may be final: /b p d t g k v f ð θ z s ž š m n ŋ l r/   (19)
VV that may be initial: /aɪ aʊ ɔɪ/   (3)
VV that may be final: /aɪ aʊ ɔɪ/   (3)
CC that may be initial: /bl br pl pr dr dw tr tw gl gr gj gw kl kr kj kw fl fr fj θr θw sp st sk sm sn sl sw šr/   (29)
CC that may be final: /pt ps dz ks ft sp st sk mz nd nt nz ns nš lb lp ld lt lk lv lf ls lš lm ln rb rp rd rt rg rk rv rf rθ rz rs rm rn rl/   (39)
CCC that may be initial: /spl spr spj str stj skr skj skw/   (8)
CCC that may be final: /ldž ltš ndž ntš rdž rtš/   (6)
(Discounted above are the bound morphs realized as /-d -t -θ -n -s -z -st/ which frequently appear within monosyllables but which make them dimorphic.)

Above are the limits of unmixed *V* and *C* combinations. The phonotactic rules that have been applied are that two stop-*C*'s cannot come together, nor two spirants; nor can voiced and unvoiced stops or spirants come together.

Monophonemic and diphonemic morphs, being usually ejaculatory, echoic, or phonosymbolic, are not always fully conventionalized: a number end with /ʊ ə h/ sounds which are not otherwise found finally. Nonce inventions of similar kind may produce phoneme sequences outside the usual phonotactic limits—Kipling's 'a big *schloop* of mud', for example, since /šl-/ is not in the English inventory. In the United States /šm-/, otherwise non-English, has become familiar through the introduction of many German surnames (Schmidt, Schmelzer, etc.) to the point where such words as the slang *schmoo* can be created using this new initial sequence. We may remember at this point the Old English sequences /fn- hn- hl- hr- wl- wr-/ which were lost in Middle English. The phonotactic rules themselves are subject to change.

TABLE 1. GRID FOR CV SEQUENCES

Consonant	Vowel					
	i	e	u	o	ɔ	ɑ
b	bee	bay	boo	bow		baa
p	pea	pay	pooh	po	paw	pa
d	dee	day	do	doe	daw	da
t	tee	Tay	too	toe	taw	ta!
g	ghee*	gay	goo	go	gaw	
k	key	kay	coo		caw	
v	vee					
f	fee	fay	phoo!	foe	fa'†	
ð	thee	they		though		
θ	thee‡				thaw	
z	zee		zoo			
s	see	say	soo	so	saw	
š	she	shay	shoe	show	shaw	shah*
m	me	may	moo	mow	maw	ma
n	knee	nay	new**	no	gnaw	nah!
l	lee	lay	loo	low	law	la!
r		ray	rue	row	raw	rah!
h	he	hay	who	hoe	haw	ha!
j	ye	yea	you	yo	yaw	ya!
w	we	way	woo	woe	wa'†	wah!

* foreign words not fully naturalized.
† Scots, not fully naturalized.
‡ obs., 'prosper'.
** U.S., midwestern, western, and some eastern /nu/.

TABLE 2. TYPES OF POSSIBLE PHONEME COMBINATIONS

Vowel and consonant combinations	Sample morph	Factors	Fillable slots
V	oh!	$6 (+/ə \; ʊ/)$	8
C	sh!	$11 (+/h/)$	12
VV	ow!	$(11 \times 6) + 6$	72
CC	ts!	$20 \times (19 - 6)$	260
CCC	pst!	1	1
VC	at	11×19	209
CV	to	20×6	120
VCC	ask	11×39	429
CCV	true	29×6	174
VVC	out	3×19	57
CVV	pie	20×3	60
CVC	pit	$20 \times 11 \times 19$	4,180
CCVV	spy	29×3	87
VVCC	oust	3×39	117
CVVC	boil	$20 \times 3 \times 19$	1,140
VCCC	urge	11×6	66
CVCC	fast	$20 \times 11 \times 39$	8,580
CCVC	step	$29 \times 11 \times 19$	6,061
CCCV	splay	8×6	48
CCCVC	splash	$8 \times 11 \times 19$	1,672
CVCCC	wasps	$20 \times 11 \times 6$	1,320
CCCVCC	squirt	$8 \times 11 \times 39$	3,432
CCVCCC	crunch	$29 \times 11 \times 6$	1,914
			30,019

We are now in a position to calculate the numbers of fillable slots which should appear on the grid when *C* and *V* sequences are combined in monosyllabic morphs. A relatively simple grid, that for *CV*, is seen in Table 1. Table 2 shows what combinations are possible and how many, and gives a sample word of each type. To know how many of the fillable slots are actually filled, however, one would have to see all the permissible combinations of phonemes and separate the real morphs from the unreal ones.

If all the permissible combinations were gridded thus by a computer and printed out, then the unreal combinations eliminated leaving the unfilled slots, the remainder should furnish a full inventory of the morphs of English. These could then be sorted in a number of ways, each of which would have advantages of its own. Rhyming series (vertically on the grid) and ablaut series (horizontally) would appear showing the various analogical sound patterns that exist—in effect, potential structural paradigms. Diachronic, diatopic, and diastatic comparisons would be facilitated. Psycholinguists, among others, would use the grid presentation to refine on experiments employing nonsense words, since these latter could now be chosen from unfilled slots with reference to their being more or less favored patterns, and according to their functional loads. More trivially, seekers after names for new products could know from a gridded lexicon how much analogical support any combination had—whether, therefore, it might seem to the user of the language quite natural, or on the contrary unusual or striking, if such were desired.

In sum, an ideal lexicon comprising a full inventory of the morphs and morph combinations of a language, arranged and studied structurally, is now within the realm of possibility. The grid presentation would make evident a number of relationships and structural patterns at present obscured by the nonphonemic orthography and alphabetic listing of our dictionaries. Phonotaxis itself would be better understood if, for example, one could know the numbers of morphs which utilize a given sequence. The structural pressure of paradigms could be seen in connection with patterns of word-formation. Recent work on phonosymbolism in submorphic phoneme sequences would be facilitated. Most of the features of the ordinary dictionary could be preserved—the list of forms, their grammatical classifications, pronunciation, labeling for usage, etymology, recording of sense, etc.—but the emphasis would be shifted to the structural characteristics, and a scientific description would be sought excluding, or at least clearly separating, anything not objective (e.g. involving social or esthetic judgments).

How much of the results of such a study could be fed back advantageously into the everyday dictionary would be for the dictionary-makers to judge, and would depend on their disposition toward scientific lexicography and the rate at which they could change the demands of their market. In any case, and quite apart from direct public utility, such a study would furnish a new resource for scholarship since the language would be better understood than before.

2

THE USES OF *shr* IN MANDARIN CHINESE

Kuo-Ping Chou

In this paper I propose to show that the character *shr*[1] in Chinese has grammatical and phonological functions as well as lexical meanings. I limit myself to modern colloquial usage. The character *shr* occurs with high frequency, but is not usually explained in textbooks teaching Mandarin Chinese in the United States. The main corpus is taken from two novels[2] which were written in the late 1920's and early 1930's when the Colloquial Written style was being formulated—a style that eventually became the pattern of later writers.

This was an important period in the development of Modern Chinese because the intellectuals of China made use of the novel as a less painful way to introduce to their generation Western, democratic ideas. *jyā*, which was first published in 1927, by March 1949 was in its 30th printing; *dž yè*, which was first published in 1933, by March 1951 was in its 24th printing. These numerous printings during even the war years attest to the novels' great popularity with the reading public. Today the two authors, bā jīn (Pa Chin) and máu dwèn (Mau Tun) are both important men not only in the government of Mainland China but also among Chinese writers in general. However, being propagandists first on the one hand, and on the other chiefly writers, they used sentences longer and more complex than is usually true of oral speech. Being a native speaker myself, I deem it appropriate and expedient to use simple and patterned sentences of my own (parenthetically numbered 1–24 below) to illustrate and strengthen specific points under discussion.

In the first 100 pages from each of the novels, a distributional analysis shows that the character *shr* occurs in certain positions more frequently than in others. In approximately 160,000 running characters, *shr* occurs 1,699 times: 1,060 times immediately after an adverb, 352 times immediately before a verb, 524 times immediately between two substantival units, and 391 times when it formed part of an adverb. These figures overlap (see §5).

In Chinese-English dictionaries, the modern usage of *shr* is usually translated as 'to be, yes, correct'. This study shows that the character *shr* has four uses in Mandarin Chinese. (1) When it has tertiary stress (normal-speech stress pattern), it acts as a coordinator between two substantives.

(2) When it has either primary or no stress (nonnormal-speech stress pattern), it is a preverb and gives a special emotional connotation. (3) It has a narrow area of meaning ('is so, is true'), used in making small talk. (4) Finally, *shr* seems to have a phonologic value in supplying the second syllable to the movable adverb[3] in one of its two possible positions; in its other position, the movable adverb does not have to have its suffix. The monosyllabic and disyllabic forms are in free variation in the second position.

1. [substantive *shr* substantive]—as a relatively free word (a subclass of verb) meaning 'it is,[4] it equals'.

(1) *jèi ₁₁shr̀ shū*   'This *shr* book.'

In this pattern *shr* has tertiary stress[5] and may be omitted if it is not immediately preceded by an immovable, monosyllabic adverb,[6] if its second substantive is modified, and if it is not in an initial utterance of a topic of conversation.

(2) [*wǒ ₁₁shr̀ gāuli rén*]   *tā jūnggwo rén*   '[I am a Korean]   He is a Chinese.'

We can be sure it is *shr* that is being left out in sentence (2) because if it were changed into a question by proper intonation, the answer would be *shr̀* or *búshr̀*.[7]

(3) *tā jūnggwo rén?*   'Is he Chinese?'

(4) *shr̀, shr̀ jūnggwo rén*   'Yes, he is Chinese', or
búshr̀ jūnggwo rén   'He is not Chinese.'

However, if both the preceding and the following substantives are heavily modified, the tendency is to keep *shr*.[8]

(5) *shwōhwàde neiwei syáujye shr̀ wǒ péngyoude jyéjye*   'The lady who is talking is my friend's elder sister.'

In the sentence pattern of substantive *shr* substantive, *shr* is in its most favored position. In 1,699 examples found in my data, it occurs 524 times in this position, plus 269 times preceded by an adverb which modifies it to form a predicate. In the pattern of substantive *shr* substantive, *shr* behaves like verbs in the language in being able to form a question by the regular device of inserting *bu* (negative morpheme) between two examples —*shrbushr*.[9]

(6) *tā ₁₁shrbushr̀ₐ nánjing rén? ₁₁shr̀*   'Is he a Nanking man? Yes.'

The meaning of *shr* in this pattern, however, is no more 'yes' than all affirmative verbs in answers are 'yes.' The language does not have a word for 'yes' or 'no' as in English.

2. ... ['*shr*/.*shr* ...]—as a relatively free word (a subclass of preverb) meaning 'sure, indeed'.

2.1. If *shr* should have primary stress in an otherwise identical sentence to those in §1, it expresses either strong reaffirmation of the speaker's opinion or disagreement with the listener.

(7) *tā 'shr̀ nánjing rén*   'He is a Nanking man [as I said before, in spite of what you may say].'

This looks like a simple substitution of the tertiary stress by the primary stress, but an analogous sentence shows that it is an addition of *'shr̀* with the primary stress in addition to a complete sentence; and in sentence (7) the optional $_{,,}$*shr̀* with tertiary stress is missing. Witness:

(8) *tā 'shr̀ tsūngming*   'He *is* bright.'

In the data examined, there are only three examples that, judging from the content, are clearly of this type; but since written Chinese does not indicate stress or word juncture, there is no way of ascertaining how many others are meant to be in this group and how many in the next.[10]

2.2. On the other hand, if *shr* loses stress completely, so that it becomes atonic and enclitic to either the preceding or following word, it gives a contrastive emphasis to the word it is attached to, usually correcting the listener's misunderstanding.

(9) *'tā .shr nánjing rén*   'He is a native of Nanking [not his wife].'

(10) *tā .shr 'nánjing rén*   'He is a native of *Nanking* [not Peking].'

(11) *'wǒ .shr búchyù*   '[Oh, no, not me!] I'm not going.'

In the data examined, there are 68 examples that have *shr* in addition to a complete sentence (without being preceded by an adverb), but again it is impossible to determine how many are intended to have this meaning since their written form is indistinguishable from that described in §2.1.

The stressless *shr* also occurs as part of a set expression for diplomatic refusal of requests, and excuse or explanation of denial of mild accusations, as in

(12) *chyù .shr chyùde*   literally 'Go *shr* go *de*' but it means

'Y-e-s, true, [he] is going, b-u-t ...'

In the data there are only two examples of this kind, both of which are not followed by 'but'; however, the implication of concession is clear.

2.3. This additional *shr*, with either primary stress or no stress, may also form a question by inserting *bu* (negative morpheme) between two examples—*shrbushr*$_b$ (see note 9),

(13) *tā 'shr̀bushr̀*$_b$ *chyù?*   '*Is* he or *isn't* he going?'

(14) *tā .shrbushr*$_b$ *'chyù?*   'He *is* going, *isn't* he?'

(15) *'tā .shrbushr*$_b$ *chyù?*   '*He's* going, isn't *he?*'

The distinction is very fine. All express strong feeling, a rather rude indication of impatience. In the data, there are only three examples of *shrbushr*$_b$, but there are four other examples of this meaning in a more literary form of

shr̀ fŏu. A listener may answer in the question form, *'shr̀ma?* equivalent
to 'Is *that* so?' expressing doubt, and the first speaker may even say *'shr̀!*
equivalent to 'You bet your life it is!' Or the listener may be less impolite
and say, *.shrma* 'You don't say.' He does not really care one way or another.

2.4. The properties of *shr* discussed in §2 lead me to conclude that *shr*,
with primary stress or no stress at all, is a preverb and therefore in the same
class as *béng* 'need not', *byé* 'do not', *děi* 'have to', *găn* 'dare to', *hwèi*
'know how to', *kěn* 'consent to', *kéyi* 'have permission to', *néng* 'be able
to', etc. Like these, neither *'shr̀* nor *.shr* may occur in initial utterances
without a verb of another class.[11] Neither may be immediately preceded by
bu (negative morpheme), nor be accompanied by aspect participles.

3. [*'shr!/.shrma?*]—as a free word (a subclass of verb) or a complete
utterance meaning 'yes, uh-huh, I see, oh?'
    There are a few isolated situations where *shr* is still used as assent with-
out a previous question containing *shr*. A Manchu servant is extremely
polite and always says *shr* to everything his master has to say. This is also
true in the armed forces where the standard answer to all orders from those
of higher rank is *'shr̀!* similar to the U.S. Navy's 'Aye, aye, sir!' Aside from
these situations, one rarely hears *shr* as 'yes' nowadays. In the data examined, there is one example that is used as assent, where the question
does not contain *shr*, spoken by a maid answering her mistress. There are,
however, seven examples where *shr̀* and *búshr̀* are used in reported speech,
e.g. 'I answered a *shr̀* and left immediately.'
    On the other hand, *shrde*[12] to indicate agreement is fairly common, and is
usually at the beginning of a speech, whether or not the previous speech is
in the form of a question, e.g. ₁₁*shr̀de, wŏ* ₁₁*shr̀ ge nwòrwòde rén* 'Yes, I am a
weakling.' In the data examined, there are 17 examples, only one of which
is in the middle of a speech, where the speaker wishes to be very dramatic.
The interesting point is that all 17 examples occur in one of the books
(*jyā*), which also gives a variant form ₁₁*shr̀.a* (seven examples):[13] ₁₁*shr̀.a,
tā bú ywànyi chyù* 'That's it; he isn't willing to go.' The other book contains three examples of this variant. The use of these forms, *shrde* and
shr.a, with the tertiary stress at the beginning of a speech is a rhetorical
device. Often, as in the examples mentioned above, the agreement comes
without being solicited.
    Sometimes, the question *shrbushr*₍ (see note 9) or *shrma* or *ní shwō
.shrbushr* 'You say *shrbushr*' is tacked on after a completed opinion when
the speaker wishes to appear to include the listener in the conversation;
the construction closely resembles the French *n'est-ce pas*. Such a question
causes the listener to say *'shr̀*, ₁₁*shr̀.a*, or ₁₁*shr̀de* occasionally, like the Eng-

lish 'yes' when listening to a long telephone monologue. The speaker may express his opinion in a long utterance consisting of many sentences, or in a short utterance consisting of one or two words.

(16)   *nǐ chyù, .shrbushr₀?*   'You are going, aren't you?'

This rhetorical-question form where an affirmative response is expected, though not obligatory, is associated with a small group of similar expressions:

(17)   *nǐ chyù, chéngbuchéng?*   'Will it do if you go?'
(18)   *nǐ chyù, kéyibukéyi?*   'Will it be all right if you go?'
(19)   *nǐ chyù, syíngbusyíng?*   'Will it do if you go?'
(20)   *nǐ chyù, dwèibudwèi?*   'Is it correct that you are going?'
(21)   *nǐ chyù, hǎubuhǎu?*   'How about your going?'

The answer to these questions may be either affirmative or negative, although the speaker expects confirmation: *shr, cheng, keyi, sying, dwei,* and *hau*, respectively.[14]

There are thus three degrees of certainty.

(22)   *nǐ chyùbuchyù* or *nǐ chyù ma?*   'Are you going?'

is a genuine question with no previous information implied (§1).

(23)   *nǐ shrbushrᵦ chyù* or *nǐ shr chyù ma?*   'Are you or aren't you going?'

With either primary or no stress, this is a repeat question. The problem has come up before, and the questioner wants a definite answer, rather expecting the affirmative (§2).

(24)   *nǐ chyù ‖shr̂bushr̂₀* or *nǐ chyù, ‖shr̂ma?*   'You are going, aren't you?'

is a rhetorical question. The speaker is quite sure that you are going (§3).

4. [-*.shr*]—as a derivative suffix supplying the second syllable to certain monosyllabic adverbs. This suffixing occurs only to movable adverbs. In the data examined there are 1,060 examples of *shr* or *bushr* immediately preceded by adverbs; of these, 566, distributed among 54 different adverbs, are movable; and 494, distributed among 38 different adverbs, are immovable.

4.1. Some movable adverbs are disyllabic, while others have free variants which are monosyllabic. A detailed analysis of the distribution of movable adverbs[15] with *shr* in the data follows.

4.1.a. *shr* appears as a suffix in 12 movable adverbs, 11 of which may occur without the suffix in one of the two positions where the movable adverbs may occur—after the subject where the predominantly monosyllabic immovable adverb may also occur.

These 12 adverbs can again be broken down into three groups. In the

first group, there is only one adverb, *yúshr* 'thereupon' (67 examples).
It never occurs without *shr* in either position. *shr* is an integral part of the
adverb.

There are six adverbs in the second group. Each has two allomorphs,
one of which has *shr* as a suffix. When these adverbs occur after the subject
or without the subject, they often appear without the suffix. When *shr*
does follow, it is often the verb of the utterance, and not the suffix of the adverb. This is very clear when *shr* is negated. However, the lexical meanings
of the adverbs do not change whether they are in the first or second position. These adverbs are: *kĕshr* 'however' (134 examples), *dànshr* 'however'
(69 examples), *dzŭngshr* 'without exception' (28 examples), *yàushr* 'if'
(26 examples), *rwòshr* 'if' (2 examples), *dānshr* 'alone, singly' (3 examples).

The third group comprises 5 adverbs that have homophonic immovable
adverbs with different lexical meanings. They also have two allomorphs
each. When they occur immediately before the verb, they often drop the
suffix. These are: *jřshr* 'only' (30 examples), *jyòushr* 'even though, even
if' (13 examples), *byànshr* 'even though, even if' (8 examples), *háishr* 'it is
better that ...' (17 examples), *dàushr* 'unexpectedly' (3 examples).

Thus, these 12 adverbs always have *shr* as an integral part of the word
when they occur before the subject (324 out of 391 occurrences), and all
but one may omit *shr* when they occur after the subject (67 occurrences),
especially if the following verb is negated.

4.1.b. Two other adverbs seem to be in a stage of fluctuation. *hwòshr*,
with its free variants *hwò*, *hwòjě*, and *yíhwò* 'or' has 12 examples in my
data. In four of the sentences where the verb *shr* is called for, the authors
use two rather literary forms in order to avoid *hwòshr ˌˌshř*. In three sentences containing *hwòjě*, two are followed by the preverbal *shr* (§2) and
one by the intersubstantival *shr* (§1); and in another sentence where *yíhwò*
(very literary) is used it is followed by the intersubstantival *shr*. The
remaining eight examples have *hwòshr* as an adverb. The other fluctuating
construction is *érshř* with its free variant *fănérshř* 'on the contrary' (eight
examples). Its function is to contrast the second clause with the first. In
two of these sentences, the first clause is in the negative and the second
clause is introduced by *ershr*; in five, the first clause is in the affirmative
and the second clause has *erbushr*. The remaining example has a disyllabic
adverb *faner*. In all these sentences the subject of the second clause is not
present and *shr* is an intersubstantival verb. The adverb here is *faner* or
er, not *fanershř* or *ershř*. It is followed by the verb *shr*.

4.1.c. The remaining 40 movable adverbs account for 146 examples.
They are always disyllabic; none of them has *shr* as part of the adverb;
and when *shr* follows, as it does in all these examples, it is a verb, either
intersubstantival or preverbal.

4.1.d. The distribution of *shr* in connection with movable adverbs can be summarized as follows. (1) Twelve adverbs accounting for 400 examples,[16] all but one having two allomorphs (with or without *shr*), appear only 17 times without suffix *shr* (13 times as preverb and 4 times as intersubstantival verb). (2) Two fluctuating adverbs account for 20 examples. One has four allomorphs, one of which has *shr* as a suffix (eight examples). The other has two allomorphs, one of which is disyllabic but not with *shr* as suffix. (3) Forty other movable adverbs accounting for 146 examples are disyllabic without *shr* as suffix, but all of them are followed by the verb *shr* (113 times as intersubstantival verb). Thus, the structure of Modern Chinese apparently requires a movable adverb before a subject to be nonmonosyllabic,[17] and *shr* is used as a suffix.

4.2. The situation is different for immovable adverbs, which never occur before the subject. In an initial utterance, they may immediately precede any part of the predicate except the normal object and the sentence particle.[18] They never occur in the final position of the sentence, as they are always in close juncture with the following word, often the verb. In the data, only those followed by *shr* are analyzed. All but three are monosyllabic. All cover a much wider area of lexical meaning than English adverbs and are extremely difficult to translate. There are 494 examples of *shr* immediately preceded by 38 different immovable adverbs.[19] In 352 of these, *shr* is a preverb, followed by another verb; in the remaining 142, it is an intersubstantival verb, followed by a nominal unit. None of the examples in the data has *shr* as a suffix to the adverb. Thus, the structure of Modern Chinese does not appear to require the immovable adverb to be non-monosyllabic as long as it can form a pronounceable unit with the verb which always follows.

TABLE 1. DISTRIBUTIONAL ANALYSIS OF THE USES OF *shr*

Section in paper	S*shr*S*	Preverb	Adverb suffix	Miscellaneous	Number of examples in data	
					By subsection	By section
1.	524					524
2.1		3			3	
2.2		68		2	70	
2.3		7			7	80
3.				35	35	35
4.1.a	4	13	383		400	
4.1.b	10	2	8		20	
4.1.c	113	33			146	
4.2	142	352			494	1,060
Total	793	478	391	37	—	1,699

* S = substantive.

4.3. The figure 1,060 includes: from the group of movable adverbs, 48 occurrences as preverbs (not recounted in the figure 352), 127 occurrences between two substantival units (not recounted in the figure 524), 391 occurrences forming part of an adverb (recounted); and from the immovable adverbs, 352 occurrences as preverbs (recounted), and 142 occurrences between two substantival units (not recounted in the figure 524).

5. Table 1 summarizes the four uses of the character *shr* in Mandarin Chinese, as determined by a study of the first 100 pages of two different novels in which *shr* occurs 1,699 times in approximately 160,000 running characters.

NOTES

1 Y. R. Chao and L. S. Yang, *Concise dictionary of spoken Chinese* (Cambridge, Mass., 1947); H. A. Giles, *A Chinese-English dictionary*, 2nd ed. rev. and enl. (Shanghai, 1912); R. H. Mathews, *A Chinese-English dictionary* no. 5794 (Cambridge, Mass., 1950). Mathews and Giles use *shih*[4] (romanizations in the latter following the Wade-Giles system), Chao and Yang write *shyh*, and Chinese linguists at Yale University write *shr̀*. I have chosen to use the Yale spelling system so that I can indicate the tone when I need to and reserve the superscripts for the notes. As the function of *shr* depends greatly on the degree of stress, I shall use the unmarked *shr* for the character.
2 *jyā* (*Chia* 'The family') by bā jīn (Pa Chin, pen name of Li Fei-kan, born in the southwestern Mandarin speech area), 30th printing (Kai Ming, 1949); and *dž yè* (*Tzu Yeh* 'Twilight' or 'Midnight') by máu dwèn (Mao Tun, pen name of Shen Yen-ping, born in Hangchow which is Wu phonemically but Mandarin lexically), 24th printing (Kai Ming, 1951).
3 Chinese adverbs are of two kinds: movable and immovable. Movable adverbs may occur either before or after the subject; immovable adverbs may not occur before the subject. Both kinds must occur before the verb.
4 Although the substantives may be phrases or clauses, as in English, the Chinese sentence pattern does not include a substantive-verb-adjective sequence; *shr* therefore does not occur between substantive and adjective, as in *tā tsūngming* 'He is bright.' Elsewhere I have used [N₁ *shr* N₁]—two substantives having the same referent. I am grateful to Samuel E. Martin for his suggestion to include 'it' in *shr* to cover such sentences as *wŏ shr̀ èr máu chyán* 'As to me (mine), it was twenty cents.'
5 There are four degrees of stress: primary ('), secondary (ₗ), tertiary (ₗₗ), and zero (. or no mark). In this paper the stress is marked only when it is relevant to the point under discussion.
6 Most immovable adverbs are monosyllabic. Since Modern Chinese does not favor monosyllabic words, these adverbs are usually followed either by other adverbs or by the verb in close juncture; or they may be made disyllabic by the suffix *shr*, discussed in §4.

7   In Chinese, the answer always includes the verb if the question contains a verb, i.e. except when the question is something like 'Who?' where the answer would be 'Me'. A question such as 'Do you go to school?' requires 'Go' or 'Not go' as the answer. *bu* is a negative morpheme, which negates whatever it precedes.

8   In the Written Colloquial (*Pai Hua*) *shr* is usually retained.

9   As there are three expressions which are represented by the same characters, subscripts have been used in order to distinguish them. ₁₁*shr̀bushr*ₐ asks a normal question (sentence patterns in §1); '*shr̀bushr̀*ᵦ or .*shrbushr*ᵦ asks a repeat question (§2); .*shrbushr*ᶜ asks a rhetorical question for the sake of courtesy (§3).

10 Aurally a native speaker would have no difficulty in distinguishing the types described in §§2.1 and 2.2.

11 By the nature of the meaning of this particular *shr*, it is never in an initial utterance, and in any event this *shr* does not precede ₁₁*shr* (§1), because the careful speaker or writer is likely to avoid two homophonic morphemes in close proximity.

12 *de* is a modifier-marking particle in the order: modifier-*de*-modified, 'that which is so'.

13 *a* is a final particle that softens and makes more informal whatever it is attached to. These formations with the particles are not unique with *shr*. For example: *hǎubuhǎu.a* 'How are you?' or 'How about it?' *hǎu, hǎude*, or *hǎu.a* 'Fine.' *dwèibudwèi.a?* 'Is it right?' *dwèi.a* 'It's right!' But the answer to *jèi shr̀bushr̀ dwèide?* is *shr̀*, not *dwèide*.

14 A negative answer is hardly ever given for the question in sentence (21). If the request cannot be granted, an expression involving *shr* is used; see §2.2.

15 Free combinations dealing with time, such as *jīntyān* 'today', *míngtyān* 'tomorrow', and with location, such as *jèr* or *jèi li* 'here' or *nèr* or *nà li* 'there' have not been included in the calculations; but indivisible words such as *syàndzài* 'now', *jìnlai* 'recently' are included.

16 Six of these are responsible for 354 examples.

17 This is also true of the suffix *-rán* which was a morpheme meaning 'in the manner of' but which is now affixed to several movable adverbs: *swéiran* 'although', *jìran* 'since', *dżran* 'naturally', *dāngran* 'of course', *gwǒran* 'as expected'. The data contain 20 such examples, where another morpheme must be added in order to have the meaning of 'in the manner', e.g. *dāngran jèiyang* 'of course it is so.' These adverbs are now well established as being disyllabic, and also usually appear with the suffix in the second position.

18 Normally the object comes after the verb, and therefore the adverb cannot precede it immediately because all adverbs must precede the verb.

19 Nine of the 38 adverbs are responsible for 378 examples.

3

THE ESTABLISHMENT
OF A VERBAL BASE FORM FOR ARABIC

Jon L. Erickson

In the description and presentation of the verbal system of a language, it is useful to be able to establish some base form which can serve as a stable point of departure for the derivation of the verbal system as a whole and which can serve both as the citation form, when it is desirable to cite a verb qua verb, and as the main verbal entry in a lexicon of the language. In English, the uninflected verb stem occurs widely and is readily available for use as a base form. In Arabic, however, the uninflected stem does not occur, and if a base form is to be selected, it must be chosen either from among inflected forms—none of which can properly be called an infinitive— or from among various artificial forms constructed on one basis or another. It is the purpose of the present note to discuss the merits and disadvantages of selecting from among the possible base forms and to propose the adoption of a type of base form not previously employed in the description of Arabic.

Before moving into the discussion proper it will be useful to review the general characteristics of Arabic verbal morphology so as to be able to establish criteria for judging the several possible base forms. In Arabic, the verb stem co-occurs with a bi-aspectual paradigm, the two aspects usually being termed 'perfective' and 'imperfective'. Aspect is marked both by the inflectional paradigm and the structure of the stem. The verb stem is an intercalation of two discontinuous elements—a consonantal root, which carries the basic lexical meaning, and a vocalic stem formative. In Classical Arabic, canonical forms of the perfective and imperfective stem variants are *CvCvC-* and *-CCvC-*, respectively, where *C* represents the root consonants, and *v* the vowel(s) of the stem formative. The consonantal root $\sqrt{\text{ktb}}$ 'write' for example, is intercalated with *a-a* to form the perfective stem variant *katab-* and with *u* to form the imperfective variant *-ktub-*.[1] The first vowel of the perfective variant is a morphologically predictable cluster-breaker. The second vowel of the perfective (the stem vowel proper) and the stem vowel of the imperfective may be *a*, *i*, or *u*, depending on the root, but the same vowel need not appear in both aspects and the vowel of one aspectual variant is not reliably predictable from that of the other.[2]

A verbal base form muts therefore, provide information concerning, the consonantal root and the aspectually variable stem vowels. Any additional information is superfluous in a base form. The grammar can be expected to provide for the inflectional system and to supply rules for the derivation of all inflected verbal forms.

Traditionally, because of reluctance to go beyond attested forms in search of a verbal base, Arabists have usually selected the third-person masculine singular of the perfective as base form. Thus, a form like *kataba* (lit. 'he wrote') is used for citation and glossed simply as 'write'. Though this procedure avoids the problems of using an artificial base, it has little to recommend it. Such a base form (like any inflected form which might be selected) provides more linguistic information than is desirable—information that properly belongs in the grammar—thus necessitating the inaccurate and misleading gloss. The use of *kataba* would also seem to argue covertly for some sort of grammatical priority for the perfective, and, in particular, for the third-person masculine singular of the perfective, though there is nothing to support such priority. The form, moreover, does not supply any information as to the stem vowel of the imperfective; and it is thus necessary to have additional information before such a form can be used in conjunction with the grammar to derive the full verbal system. This last deficiency may be offset by appending the stem vowel of the imperfective (by means of parentheses or some such device) to the citation form, but such a procedure presents a base form that lacks compactness.

As an alternative to using inflected forms, Arabists have at times made use of various artificial base forms. For example, the abstracted verbal root followed by some notation as to stem vocalization, e.g. $\sqrt{\text{ktb}}$ *a/u* 'write', may be used in place of the more conventional base form of the type *kataba*. As a second possibility, either the perfective or imperfective stem variant may be used as base with the alternative stem vowel being appended, e.g. *katab-* (*u*) or *-ktub-* (*a*). Both possibilities meet the demand that the base form should supply full information as to both verbal root and stem vocalization. Both, as well, supply no superfluous grammatical information and thus could be glossed accurately as base forms. The first (i.e. $\sqrt{\text{ktb}}$ *a/u* 'write'), however, is both noncompact and unpronounceable as a form, and is thus unwieldy. The second—the use of the uninflected stem—while more readily pronounceable, is also noncompact, and the hyphens emphasize its lack of completeness as a form. If the second possibility is selected, moreover, it is still necessary to come to grips with the problem of assigning grammatical priority to one or the other of the verbal aspects.

To the disadvantages, both of the inflected and of the artificial forms discussed above, there would appear to be one alternative: the construction of a special verbal base form which would avoid the above difficulties; and this can be done with no great difficulty. Using the characteristically Arabic morphological process of intercalation, it is possible to take the consonantal root and a stem formative compounded of the two aspectual stem vowels and produce a very serviceable base form: e.g. $\sqrt{\text{ktb}}$ plus a/u would yield the base form *katub 'write'. A similar base form could be constructed for each verb:[3]

STEM VARIANTS	BASE FORMS
jalas-; imperf. -jlis-	*jalis 'sit'
ɣarab-; imperf. -ɣrub-	*ɣarub 'depart'
sarib-; imperf. -srab-	*sirab 'flow'

Given a citation form like *katub 'write', a grammar of Classical Arabic would stipulate that in co-occurrence with the perfective paradigm *katub would yield katab-. The first vowel of the base form indicates that the stem vowel of the perfective is a. (The first vowel of the perfective, as stated earlier, is predictable.) In co-occurrence with the imperfective paradigm, *katub would yield -ktub-, the second vowel of the base form indicating that the stem vowel of the imperfective is u. The indicative paradigm of *katub 'write' will serve as illustration:

*katub + perfective		*katub + imperfective
	first person	
katab-tu	sing.	ʔa-ktub-u
katab-na:	pl.	na-ktub-u
	second person	
katab-ta	masc. sing.	ta-ktub-u
katab-ti	fem. sing.	ta-ktub-iyna
katab-tuma:	du.	ta-ktub-a:ni
katab-tum	masc. pl.	ta-ktub-uwna
katab-tunna	fem. pl.	ta-ktub-na
	third person	
katab-a	masc. sing.	ya-ktub-u
katab-at	fem. sing.	ta-ktub-u
katab-a:	masc. du.	ya-ktub-a:ni
katab-ata:	fem. du.	ta-ktub-a:ni
katab-uw	masc. pl.	ya-ktub-uwna
katab-na	fem. pl.	ya-ktub-na

Modern Cairo Arabic can be used to illustrate how the same type of verbal base form can be constructed for other (i.e. non-Classical) varieties of Arabic. The Cairo Arabic verb also displays the aspectually variable stem vowel:

STEM VARIANTS	BASE FORMS
daras(-); imperf. *-dris*(-)	*daris 'study'
nizil(-); imperf. *-nzil*(-)	*nizil 'descend'
daxal(-); imperf. *-dxul*(-)	*daxul 'enter'

The base forms are not necessarily identical with those of Classical Arabic, but are built on exactly the same principle, the intercalation of the consonantal root and the aspectual stem vowels. Given the Cairo base form *katib, the grammar would stipulate that in co-occurrence with the perfective paradigm *katib would yield *katab*(-); with the imperfective, *-ktib*(-). The first vowel of the perfective is again predictable, though on a different basis from that of classical Arabic.[4] The following paradigm for Cairo Arabic may be compared with that given above for Classical Arabic:

*katib + perfective		*katib + imperfective
	first person	
katab-t	sing	*ʔa-ktib*
katab-na	pl.	*ni-ktib*
	second person	
katab-t	masc.	*ti-ktib*
katab-ti	fem.	*ti-ktib-i*
katab-tu	pl.	*ti-ktib-u*
	third person	
katab	masc.	*yi-ktib*
katab-it	fem.	*ti-ktib*
katab-u	pl.	*yi-ktib-u*

Such a constructed base form is completely serviceable for Arabic and lacks the disadvantages both of the inflected forms and the more familiar artificial forms. It provides full information about both consonantal root and aspectual stem vowels. It supplies none of the superfluous grammatical information offered by an inflected form, and it removes the necessity of choosing between perfective and imperfective base forms since, as a form, it is aspectually neutral. It is typographically compact and complete, and since it conforms to regular Arabic morphological patterns, it is easily pronounceable and readily understood and remembered. Such a form might also be extremely useful in teaching Arabic to non-Arabic speakers and in facilitating the teaching of Standard Arabic to nonstandard speakers since it would remove the most important ambiguity in Arabic verbal morphology—the prediction of the opposite aspectual stem vowel.

Given the morphological and morphophonemic rules that would necessarily be found in the grammars of each variety of Arabic, all of the attested verbal forms can be derived directly from the proposed base form. The special construct could provide Arabic with a verbal base form comparable to the base forms in other languages, making it simpler to cite a verb qua verb and providing for a more compact, economical, and useful primary verbal entry in the lexicon. As a form, the proposed construct is admittedly artificial, but no more artificial than, say, the commonly accepted citations of the abstracted consonantal root, i.e. $\sqrt{\text{ktb}}$, $\sqrt{\text{jls}}$, etc. The independent root does not occur in the language, but its abstraction and citation as an entity are illuminating for the description of Arabic, and, as a result, Arabists have never hesitated to make use of it. The proposed base form is defensible on similar grounds of utility.

NOTES

1 Upon this basic stem may also be built a series of regularly derived secondary stems.

2 A traditional rule of thumb states that if the perfective stem vowel is u, the imperfective is also u; if i, then a. If the perfective is a, however, the imperfective may be a, i, or u: u is the most common; i generally occurs if C_2 or C_3 is l or r; a generally occurs if C_2 or C_3 is a glottal or pharyngeal. See M. Gaudefroy-Demombynes and R. Blachere, *Grammaire de l'arabe classique* 41 (Paris, 1952).

3 The verbs used for illustration are all formed upon 'strong' or regular roots. Roots where $C_2 = C_3$ (doubled roots) or those where one or more of the root consonants is w or y (weak roots) require special morphophonemic rules to produce the actually attested forms from the canonical forms, e.g. *marra* < *marara* 'he passed by', imperf. *yamurru* < *yamruru* or *qa:la* < *qawala* 'he said', imperf. *yaquwlu* < *yaqwulu. But since such rules would operate on the aspectual canonical forms, not on the base forms themselves, the base forms would still be of the form *marur* 'pass by' and *qawul* 'say', just as they would be for verbs formed on strong roots.

4 In Classical Arabic, the vowel is predictable on the basis of voice—agentive or nonagentive; in Cairo Arabic the first vowel of the perfective has the same quality as the stem vowel.

4

LANGUAGE,
APPROXIMATION, AND EXTENDED TOPOLOGIES

Preston C. Hammer

In the theories of formal languages, recursive functions, Turing machines, and automata there are attempts to apply mathematical methods to linguistics. Since these theories are already extensive I do not propose to discuss them here. Instead I will present a few considerations which I believe are important in understanding certain aspects of language. These considerations cannot now be dignified by the name of a theory, but my mathematical system of extended topology, independent of its application to linguistics, may now be said to be a theory.

I have been working on extended topology intermittently since 1951, and eventually propose to generate an open-ended mathematical system which will embrace all formal systems. The job is already well started in that several fundamental concepts and a significant body of theory are available. The evolutionary stage of my thinking has reached that of relation theory where various entities such as elements, sets, and classes of sets may be the related items. This stage was attained by progressing from topology to set-valued set functions, then to binary relations among sets, and to arbitrary relations among sets. From reading any of some twenty of my papers,[1] neither mathematician nor linguist might gather the impression that extended topology deals with matters of importance in linguistics.

I could claim that, since semigroups, graphs, automata, and formal languages are systems, they belong to extended topology. This is true but it is not useful. In this paper I propose to demonstrate two aspects of the relationship between linguistics and extended topology. The one aspect concerns the use of the sense of common language to generate useful concepts, i.e. linguistics can be helpful in the study of mathematics. The second aspect is the application of topological terminology to language theory. I appreciate the fact that what I have to say is informal and hence, in a way, metalinguistic. This will not, I trust, destroy its value.

LINGUISTICS AND MATHEMATICAL CONCEPTS. There are so many riches contained in the common languages that they are often ignored. Nowhere else have I seen the admission by any mathematician that he owes to the language he speaks certain fundamental notions and that he has it as the vehicle for his more technical language. In an analysis of the progress I have made in extended topology since 1951, I find that much of it came from an 'ear' keenly attuned to the common language. The slowness of my progress was due to some appreciable extent to the encrustation of general meanings of concepts in the rigid mathematical contexts which I had learned.

As an outstanding example, I select the concept of 'continuity'. The word 'continuity' is one noun derived from the adjective 'continuous' which comes from the Latin. Perhaps its entry into English was via French. Sometime in the early nineteenth century the French mathematician Augustin Louis Cauchy (1789–1857) is said to have adapted the words 'continuity' and 'continuous' for specific mathematical use when he applied them to a condition of number-valued functions. The definition given by Cauchy was the basis for subsequent mathematical definitions and extensions. In particular the Italian mathematician Giuseppe Peano (1858–1932), a founder of a form of symbolic logic, introduced the so-called epsilon-delta treatment of continuity. This treatment has been used extensively by formalists and it has not been a source of pleasure to many students of calculus.

The abstraction of geometry and analysis in topology following the introduction of set theory by the German mathematician Georg Cantor (1845–1918) led to a generalization of the concept of continuity to the abstract spaces of topology. These generalizations proved quite fruitful, although many mathematicians regarded them as generalizations for the sake of generalization. The amount of effort that has gone into applications of the topological continuity concept is almost incredible. Nevertheless, when I began to consider the concept of continuity, I found the state of affairs highly unsatisfactory. A series of clues developed which gradually indicated the directions that I must follow.

The concept of continuity in 1951, insofar as I could detect, had not been fruitfully applied to situations in which there were only FINITE sets involved. Thus it was permissible to speak of a real-valued function of a real variable as being continuous; it was not permissible to speak of continuity of a function which associated integers with integers. Nevertheless, I was aware that ALGEBRAISTS used the word 'homomorphism' to describe OPERATION-PRESERVING transformations where the operations often were the usual binary ones such as multiplication and addition. On the other hand certain TOPOLOGISTS also used the word 'homomorphism' as a substitute for 'continuous function'. I decided that these two seemingly disconnected uses of the word 'homomorphism' may have arisen because there was an underlying similarity between the finite algebraic concept and the infinite topological one.

In retrospect, I cannot see how I could have stumbled about, as I did, for the next ten years after having made this latter observation. The difficulty I had was due to prejudice and habit. I could have studied the common-language concept of continuity with profit but this would not have resolved the mathematical problem of finding a MATHEMATICAL definition.

On several occasions I obtained generalizations that were exciting, but each time homomorphisms of algebra remained beyond the pale. Finally, I found that all topological homomorphisms could be included in mappings which preserved certain ORDERED binary relations among sets. Within a short time I had a tentative definition of continuity as follows: If a function preserves a relation among sets then it is, in that regard, continuous. The special relations I first chose were only restricted to ANCESTRAL ones. All at once I had included algebraic homomorphisms in set-relation preserving transformations and topological homomorphisms in the same framework.[2]

I now had a better background for seeing the importance of the continuity concept. Although I now have several possible definitions of continuity for mathematical consumption, I have also closed the gap between the common-language concept and the mathematical one. The common-language concept is the more general. What I have decided is that CONTINUITY and INVARIANCE are dual concepts. This observation is of great importance for mathematics, especially now that I have given some mechanisms to implement it. Let me quote from the second edition (1934) of *Webster's new international dictionary:* '*Continuity* signifies identity with respect to a series of changes.' That is, of course, a time-related way of saying that continuity and invariance are dual! Had I looked at this definition in 1951 I would probably have thought that it had no connection with the mathematical concept.

But what has 'continuity', which has now been so enriched in the mathematical sense, to do with language theory? The preceding discussion illustrates my decision to take two distinct uses of one word, 'homomorphism', to suggest a common basis (which is not consciously available). But I picked this illustration rather than several others for another reason. Continuity also is important in approximation theory and hence in linguistics. In the following section I will pursue this connection.

In summary, let me emphasize the nature of the work leading to a new definition of continuity. Heretofore the mathematical concept, while applying to a strategic set of mathematics problems, was remote from the common language. It virtually required infinite sets and its meanings were buried in technicalities. I have attempted both to enhance the scope of the mathematical concepts but also to show where my mathematical definitions have fallen short of common usage.

/ The following lessons are derived. First, 'continuity' is a TYPE concept— there is no intrinsic way of defining it but various applications suggest various particular instances. Next, the observation that invariance and continuity are dual should be helpful in classifying mathematical systems. In 1872 Felix Klein announced his famed 'Erlanger Program' in which he proposed to classify geometries by groups of transformations, leaving their fundamental properties invariant. This notion may now be applied more widely. Finally, the generalization of continuity in effect makes the term more AMBIGUOUS, i.e. there are now many more special instances of continuity. Of critical importance for application to linguistics is the fact that the new concepts apply well to finite sets.

APPROXIMATION, LINGUISTICS, AND CONTINUITY. It was a fortunate circumstance that I was actively interested in computing, numerical analysis, and convexity at the same time that I was developing the underlying theory of extended topology. It is true that the world of mathematics has become sufficiently complex that a person may work in it without being aware of any relevance exterior to mathematics. It is also true, however, that the most significant work, from the standpoint of society is that which has direct or indirect applications. Mathematicians immersed in the world of mathematics often come to the point of view that they have gone beyond the reach of applications and that they are independent of the matters of this world. A better-reasoned point of view is that such mathematicians are effectively at the mercy of earlier mathematicians who set down the principles before them. Independence is never complete in any case. We all live by the sufferance and connivance of our fellow humans.

When I first encountered it, approximation theory was being relegated by some Russian mathematicians and others to being a branch of linear space theory which is relegated to the field of functional analysis. The reader need understand none of this technical terminology. The point is that approximation had become so cluttered with techniques that its nature was hidden. My thoughts concerning approximation developed along with those on extended topology. To show why these two areas are actually not remote I mention that the word 'approximation' indicates CLOSENESS or PROXIMITY, whereas the principal business of topology is the study of closeness relations and space structures. Thus the beautiful neighborhood terminology of topology has this sort of meaning: A set X is CLOSE to a point p provided X meets every neighborhood (set) of p.

My researches into the numerical solution of differential equations then suggested that the usual measures of CLOSENESS of two functions were too restricted for use in numerical analysis. Why should it always be necessary to state that if one function is a good approximation to another that the other is a good approximation to the one? Why should a function be considered as a good approximation of itself? When I decided that these conditions were not necessary nor even always useful, I was prompted to extend approximation theory until I reached 'continuity' and language theory.

The end result of an approximation process is the replacement of one entity (which may itself be a set) by another. Thus I suddenly saw that approximation embraces all attempts to represent, to model, or to simulate. From the use of the common noun as a tag, to the construction of physical theories, from the imitation of a mimic to election of representatives, we are engaged in approximation processes. Vague generalities? Perhaps. But I can point to specific problems in mathematics which arose from this point of view. In particular, I refer to the concept of differential equivalence of functions and syntonicity of function pairs.[3]

The connection with matters of specific linguistic interest is now simple. Consider a translation of a book or article from one language to another. The translated work is an APPROXIMATION to the original. How shall the merit of the translation be gauged? Suppose you decide on certain important features of the original which must be preserved. If the translation preserves these features and meets other criteria, you may determine that it was a GOOD TRANSLATION. If you say that the transformation (act of translation) is good, I say that this is equivalent to saying it is CONTINUOUS! An APPROXIMATION to an entity is good when it preserves the essentials (e.g. information, structure, relationships, meanings, phonics). The difficulties in mechanical translation of languages are difficulties in approximation. Which kinds of translations are most difficult? I would estimate that poetry in general would be very difficult since it involves form, semantics, and phonics.

There is no theoretical reason why mechanical translation is not possible. The actual difficulty is in ECONOMICALLY imitating the large number of intricate correspondences used by translators. Mathematical and scientific literature should be comparatively simple to translate, in general, because the main criterion is preservation of information. Clarity of style might be required even if the original did not possess it, but this is a creative aspect of translation.

THE EFFECTIVENESS OF LANGUAGE. Some people, particularly academicians, are carried beyond the bounds of reason when they speak of the effectiveness and power of language. This kind of erroneous thinking is very widespread and it is by no means confined to teachers of language.

Actually, the attempt to describe objects in a language performs a DIS-

CONTINUOUS transformation from the object into the language—the language, being linear, is necessarily picture-destroying. For example, why are language and mathematics ineffective in describing faces or trees? I have worried about this problem at some length in connection with the problem of mechanical pattern recognition. One partial answer lies in another topological feature of language. The language is linear. This is quite rigidly true of the printed page; it is subject to debate when a language is spoken, but the basic fact remains. Suppose I were to try to describe to you my 15-year-old daughter, Kate. I doubt if I could do it well enough so that you could use the description to identify her in a collection of 200 girls. Yet, I could identify her among 50,000 or 100,000, or perhaps 10,000,000.

If the statements that we THINK in terms of our word structures (as represented in the brain) have real substance, then we have cause to consider the effect of the linear language structure on our thinking capacity. Conversely, it is becoming more and more obvious that we may well afford the attempt to have a 'language' for reading which makes better use of the eyes and to have this language independent of speech. This suggestion is but part of one which I think should be taken seriously—the re-evaluation of communication devices in terms of human physiology and psychology.

The best clue I have now to a suitable definition of dimension, which according to my interpretation is not properly defined until it applies to finite sets, involves order relations. This is of interest in computing and linguistics, although I do not yet grasp its significance. During the summer of 1964 I defined the DIMENSION (or RANK) of a partial order relation in a space to be the cardinal number of any smallest cardinal number class of linear order relations which intersect (in the squared space) to give the partial order. This definition provides the 'right' numbers for a variety of simple spaces, such as Euclidean spaces and continuous-function space. It has the enormous advantage of applying to finite sets.

The linguistic lesson here is that when we linearly order structures, not ordered nicely that way, we must impose artificial order (i.e. meaningless order) to achieve the result. To convey the information then, we must resort to devices and tricks, as well as use our brains for a place to assemble messages into meaningful messages. I find the suggestion intriguing that in the achievement of a partial order (one may take the computations of several linear orders combined for two-dimensional descriptions, for example), perhaps two distinct linear descriptions are logically equivalent to a two-dimensional one.

SUMMARY. Mathematics is a sublanguage which may benefit by thorough study of general INTENTIONS of its concepts. As an illustration, the continuity concept is shown to be much richer than mathematical treatment has suggested. The linearity of dimension of the usual spoken and printed language makes it impossible to discuss complex structures without defacing them. We need better communication devices to enable the full use of our capacities to learn. In particular, I urge the interpretations of linguistic analysis as part of an attempt to create communication devices hopefully much better suited to our physiology and psychology.

APPENDIX

FORMAL DEFINITIONS OF CONTINUITY. The preceding description, deliberately in the ordinary language, may be irritating to those who prefer formal descriptions and to whom I make the following concessions. I first define continuity in a fashion equivalent to that of topology and analysis, and proceed with the extension.

Let $t : M \to M_1$ be a mapping of a space M into a space M_1, and let the same letter indicate the induced set-valued map of all subsets of M. Let uX be the closure of X for subsets X of M and let vY be the closure of Y for subsets Y of M_1. Then t is called CONTINUOUS provided $t(uX) \subseteq v(tX)$ for all $X \subseteq M$. As a shorthand device I may write $tu \subseteq vt$ and the above definition provides topological continuity.

The very formalism $tu \subseteq vt$ suggests replacing u and v by functions other than closures of topology and also replacing t by more general set-valued set functions. None of these are parlor games, but they do provide useful restrictions on functions.

However, these generalizations refuse to embrace algebraic homomorphisms. Next, to give the example leading to the breakthrough, if ordered pairs (X_1, X_2) of sets from M are called u-associated whenever uX_1 and X_2 have a common element, then a transformation $t : M \to M_1$ is continuous if and only if t always maps u-associated pairs into v-associated pairs. From this interpretation of continuous maps as binary association-preserving I was led to ternary, n-ary, and infinite association-preserving maps. Ternary association-preserving maps then provided the maps which preserved binary operations, and I had arrived at a common definition for algebraic and topological homomorphisms.

NOTES

1 In these notes, the following references selected from my bibliography are pertinent to this paper: 'General topology, symmetry, and convexity', *Trans. of the Wisconsin academy of sciences, arts and letters*, Walter E. Scott, ed., 43.221–55 (Madison, 1955); 'Extended topology: The Wallace function of a separation', *Nieuw archief voor wiskunde* 9:3.74–86 (1961); 'Extended topology: Set valued

set functions', *Nieuw archf. wisk.* 10:3.55–77 (1962); 'Extended topology: Domain finiteness', *Indagationes mathematicae* 25:2.200–12 (1963); 'Numerical analysis as curve-fitting', *Electronische Datenverarbeitung* no. 5.223–5 (October 1963); 'Semispaces and the topology of convexity', *Proceedings of symposia in pure mathematics*, Victor L. Klee, ed., 7.305–16 (Providence, 1963); 'Extended topology: Perfect sets', *Portugaliae mathematicae* 23:1.27–34 (1964); 'Extended topology: Structure of isotonic functions', *Journal für die reine und angewandte Mathematik* Sonderabdruck, 213:3/4.174–86 (1964).

2 'Extended topology: The continuity concept', *Mathematics magazine* 36:2.101–5 (1963).

3 'Differential equivalence', *Proceedings of the international congress of mathematicians, Amsterdam*, J. C. H. Gerretson, ed., 2.226–7 (Amsterdam, 1954); 'Syntonicity of functions and the variation functional', *Rendiconti del circulo mathematico* ser. 2 vol. 8.145–51 (1959).

5

THE COMPLETION OF DESCRIPTIVE LINGUISTICS

Martin Joos

It is reported that in the 1870's a certain Patent Office examiner resigned to go into a more promising line of work because (he said) everything had been invented.

When *Readings in linguistics* was first published in 1957,[1] the descriptive linguistics which it defines was growing, as it still is today: irregularly, especially around its edges, but leaving at least one big hole inside it. To describe that hole, I must reject page 356 of *RIL* and adopt the diagram provided by George L. Trager half a dozen years before he published it in the 1956 *Encyclopædia Britannica*.[2] There were still doubtful labels and question marks in the diagram, especially because he had located the hole precisely but had not worked out a detailed theory for filling it. I completed its labeling and published it in my article 'Semology: A linguistic theory of meaning';[3] here is an extreme condensation of it:

Prelinguistics: Physiology, acoustics, etc.
> Phonology
>> Grammar (Trager's 'Morphology')
> Semology
Metalinguistics: Cultural categories of things, events, etc.

This represents any language as a tripartite mediator between the prelinguistic and the metalinguistic domain, neither of which is language. It represents its grammar as a mediator between phonology and semology, neither of which is grammar as here defined. The grammar is autonomous—not bound by any peculiarities of the real world—except that every grammar must come to terms with the one-dimensional and unidirectional nature of TIME.

Although not shown by the condensation, each of those three is again tripartite. The grammar comes to terms with time by means of one of its three subsystems, its morphophonemics, located next to the phonology; and again by means of another of them, its syntax, next to the semology. Between the syntax and the morphophonemics is the central subsystem of the grammar, its morphemics.

Except for its necessary accommodations to the nature of time, the grammar is completely autonomous: all other accommodations of the language to the nature of the physical speech process are provided for within the phonology, and all other accommodations to the nature of what is spoken of are provided for within the semology. Thus, the phonology and the semology serve to insulate the grammar from the real world so that it can be autonomous. This is a tautology: it is true by definition, for each detail within the language is assigned to one subsystem or another in a careful description in such a way as to make it true.

Prelinguistics is the same for all languages, in principle, simply because they are all spoken by the same race and by substantially the same technique; the prelinguistics can be made different only by mutilating the language, for example by deriving from it something like a writing system or what is described by George M. Cowan, 'Mazateco whistle speech'.[4]

/The metalinguistics is the same within each culture, in principle, but disparate languages hardly ever (or never) share one culture completely: there are, however, quite close approaches to that, notably among French-German bilingual natives in the Rhineland, etc., and when the approach is practically perfect we can say that the metalinguistics is the same for the two languages, meaning that the world is categorized the same no matter which language is being spoken.

Rather more interesting is the phenomenon called DIGLOSSIA, in which two disparate grammars have the same phonology and the same semology except for statistical differences.[5] Such cases demonstrate with particular clarity the essential difference between grammar and semology; within a single language that difference may be hard to discern without careful discussion, as in my semology paper. But these things are becoming clearer year by year; and the recent *Norwegian English dictionary*[6] discusses in detail and has completely exemplified that case in which the symbiosis of the two contemporary Norwegian standard languages makes them only statistically different in their phonologies, disparate in their grammars, and identical in their semologies to such an extent that a single English gloss always serves for both, with rare exceptions where a lexeme in one kind of Norwegian is accidentally unattested in the other.

The last three paragraphs form an excursus; I start again from before them. By emphasizing the morphophonemics and the syntax, and extending each of them outward over the phonology and the semology, and inward to divide the grammar between them, it becomes possible (neglecting diglossia, whistle speech, and other phenomena left unmentioned in my excursus) to describe the tripartite structure of the language as having only two parts. Then one speaks of the 'double articulation' of discourse and language as Martinet does.[7] Conversely, by redefining 'grammar' it is possible to extend its domain outward on both sides until nothing within the language (that is, nothing within it by the test that it is arbitrarily different from details of other languages) is left outside the grammar. That is the choice of the generative-transformational school. Yet the converse is not true: it is possible to treat a language as a unitary mediator between speech and reference under theories which are not transformational, or to treat it as a featureless interface as James Joyce did.[8]

There is at least one sufficient reason for preferring the tripartite description: it makes the factual hole in descriptive linguistics clearly visible, delimits it, and gives it a name of its own—SEMOLOGY. The double-articulation describers, notably the Linguistic Circle of Copenhagen, treat it as filled by their often wise but generally undocumented philosophy of the 'content plane'. The generative-transformational grammarians treat it as needing no philosophy of its own, as a featureless interface, a gap across which they throw, parallel to each other but in principle without mutual connection, an increasing number of single bridges (with such labels as 'animate' and 'passive' and 'nominalization') over which they import metalinguistics into grammar. There is so far no certainty that the number of these bridges has any limit short of the open-ended multiplicity of the metalinguistics, so that it behooves us to be patient and wait for the transformationalists to apply Ockham's Razor themselves.

Both schools, meanwhile, have been drawing upon the fragmentary knowledge of particular semologies, especially the rule-of-thumb lexical semology which appears in the subdividing of definitions in unabridged standard dictionaries. My semology paper (1958.53–70) was the first attempt to lay bare, by the traditional methods of descriptive linguistics, the theory implicit in the successful rule-of-thumb decisions, and by doing so to sketchily fill in that hole in the tripartite theory. That paper has had no published sequels as far as I know, perhaps only partly because the circulation of *Studies in linguistics* is small and I am lazy. There is at least one other possible reason which is weighty enough by itself: the enormous area that has to be covered to execute even a 1-percent-complete semology of one language (roughly, 30 pages of the latest big English dictionary, but minutely analysed and expanded to, say, 200 pages of fine print) in comparison to the year's work that will produce a 90-percent-complete grammar or the month's work for a 99-percent-complete phonology.

I have contented myself with the basic notion, there established, of the double additive-privative contribution of a lexeme to the meaning of a sentence containing it, and have carried that over into the book *The English verb: Form and meanings*.[9] This time, only the privative contribution is needed for the theory of what English verb-forms mean; whether the same would suffice elsewhere in English grammar remains moot.

One feature, and a crucial one, of the essential difference between grammar and semology is that the units, the pieces left individually unanalysed and associated with each other under the one regime or the other, are of different sizes. They correspond to different-sized segments of discourse.

In grammar, the unit is called a morpheme in American terminology, so that the morpheme may be a lexeme. The verb formula *must have shown* contains the lexeme *show*, the other morpheme -*n*, and two other segments which I find it expedient to call morphemes that are not lexemes.

In the semology of the English verb, the units are of different sizes in general. One of them agrees: *show*. But only *have* and -*n* together form one semological unit: neither means anything by itself, and -*n* here shares no meaning with the -*n* in *must be shown*. Here, then, the semological unit is more than a word or a morpheme. Conversely, the semological units which *must* imports into both formulas, the same each time, are three in number: the one morpheme imports a cluster of three allosemes, one which it shares with *ought to*, *need*, and *dare*, one which it shares with *will* or *would*, *can* or *could*, and *dare*, and one which it shares with *will* or *would*, *shall* or *should*, and *ought to*. (It shares no alloseme with *may* or *might*, the polar opposite of *must*.) Each other modal imports, similarly, an indissoluble cluster of three modal allosemes; there are six of the latter, in three polar pairs. All this is verified by the 1,340 modal occurrences in my corpus of authentic English (Joos, 1964.147–201), and no simpler theory of finite-verb meanings has been verified to my certain knowledge.

That book and that article, then, are a pair of bold attempts to bring semology under the kind of control that is usual in descriptive linguistics. They present semology as a crystalline subsystem, not an amorphous one, as phonology and grammar are already crystalline in modern descriptive linguistics; that is the only merit they can claim beyond cavil. In this sense, they constitute one 'completion' of descriptive linguistics, left standing there until someone presents an essentially better completion in due course.

But in another sense, descriptive linguistics will never be completed, any more than any other science, so that there is no reason, other than taste and temperament, to resign and go into a more promising line of work.

NOTES

1 Martin Joos, ed., *Readings in linguistics* (Washington, 1957) [4th printing; Chicago, 1966].

2 14.162E (1956). This diagram appears as Table II in the Linguistics article contributed by Trager, and was originally published in George L. Trager, *The field of linguistics* in *Studies in linguistics* occ. paper I (Norman, Okla., 1949).

3 Martin Joos, in *SIL* 13.53–70 (1958), now long out of print but again accessible as 'Language—54', *Bobbs-Merrill reprint series in languages and linguistics* (Indianapolis, 1964).

4 *Language* 24.280–6 (1948).
5 See Charles A. Ferguson, 'Diglossia', *Word* 15.325–40 (1959); William A. Stewart, 'Functional distribution of Creole and French in Haiti', *Monograph series on languages and linguistics* 15.149–59, esp. the diagram on 155, Georgetown University Institute of Languages and Linguistics (Washington, D.C., 1962); Elinor Clark Horne, *Beginning Javanese* (New Haven, 1961).
6 Einar Haugen, ed., *Norwegian English dictionary* (Madison, 1965).
7 See e.g. A. Martinet, *Elements of general linguistics* E. Palmer, trans., 22–4 (London, 1964).
8 See Martin Joos, 'Employment of the index', Appendix II in Miles L. Hanley, *Word index to James Joyce's Ulysses* (Madison, 1951).
9 Martin Joos, *The English verb: Form and meanings* 81–4 and in various other pars. (Madison, 1964).

6

PHONOLOGICAL CAUSALITY AND THE EARLY GERMANIC CONSONANTAL CONDITIONERS OF PRIMARY STRESSED VOWELS

Irmengard Rauch

1. In a recent publication on 'Indo-European [bh] > English /v/', where Murray Fowler demonstrates a principle which is part of linguistic relativity, 'that no linguistic change is unconditioned', his actual concern is the theorem derived from this principle, namely, 'that all linguistic change is phonological in origin', which, he writes, 'require[s] a reconsideration of the problem of ultimate and mediate causes.'[1] The first principle is readily acceptable from analogues in general causality theory; the second is reasonable from the fact that the phonological structure housing the change is commonly taken to be a system which by definition is a unity coherent through the interactional or interrelated functioning of its parts. De Saussure even implies that the system is a closed one, i.e. an absolute one, which suggests that although the given phonological system can undergo transformations it, as itself, remains fundamentally the same.[2]

Thus, many scholars presently occupied with phonemic change prefer to focus on the inner dynamics of the structure or mechanism embedding the conversion phenomenon. They emphasize the fact that statements about conditioners not in the particular phonological system are directly nonsignificant and often, by being prematurely or otherwise incorrectly applied, in phonemic descriptions, tend to be misleading if not erroneous relative to the actual sound phenomenon.[3]

Very likely, the understanding of the general whole imposing interdependence upon all elements, which resulted in the rejection of unconditioned or spontaneous sound change, also stimulated the limitless synthesis of speculative causal chains. Kurylowicz (1964.11) aptly notes: 'The question is where to stop when explaining ...' On the other hand, if causation is viewed anywhere within the range of infinity, then the only stopping to be had is in the form of statements which are necessarily universals. R. D. Stevick, in resurrecting the biological model, exemplifies well the satisfactory application of such an abstractive descriptive approach. He concludes:

They ['linguistic change in cultural evolution and biological evolution'] are particular developments of the general model of persistence with modification of complex systems ... linguistic change, like biological change, occurs as modification in persisting systems through selection combined with chance variation and the attendant factor of isolation, the whole [further] conditioned by population structure.[4]

As is the accepted rule, gain in completeness from working with universals is had only at the expense of obscuring individual precision, so that the question of where to stop is really a choice of working tools that are an entirely different set if particular phenomena are investigated within their actual setting alone.[5] The choice of descriptive concentration which has to be made is not one indicative of value and permanent exclusion since not any ONE approach is THE approach. Information is to be got at one time by limiting the boundaries of investigation, at another by extending them, at yet another by crossing over them, where, however, it is clear that analogies are only parallels and in no wise equations; but no useful information is obtained from at once synthesizing a unilabeled and otherwise undefined conglomerate.[6]

Consequently, reverting to the seeming banality of simply taking account of phonological realia, where and when they are found to occur within their own structure, appears to be, convincingly so, the path of least resistance in the long run for uncovering causal relationships. Such reversion has become the desired course in descriptive methodology treating sound change.

2. Traditionally it has been the habit in the reference books treating Germanic in general or Gothic, Old Norse, Old English, Old Saxon, and Old High German reference books to present the phonemes of one or more languages by means of a combined description, which is the predecessor of several exclusive techniques currently applied to phonemic inventories. Thus, in a sense, the ontogeny of phonemes was described, e.g. environmentally, derivationally, productionally. With phonemic theory, phonemic change came to mean systemic or pattern effect,[7] i.e. the change is recognized by its altering the system which itself generates the change.

Every sound change normally yields at least one segmental alteration; if the generating mechanism has a segmental reflex significantly transformed in the process of transforming another member, then there is a double systemic effect in which the overt cause is also a partial effect. In that phonological conditioners are neither necessarily segmental nor necessarily emically involved in phonemic changes the focal point in descriptions of sound changes generally has been on the primary effect, the designation of which for some changes is an arbitrarily chosen part of the approach. The exception is to be found in laryngeal scholarship, where the emphasis seems to be on the laryngeals as conditioners rather than on the phenomena produced through them.

On the other hand, if a segmental conditioner is identified and in particular if it is emically effected in the change of another phoneme, it is frequently empowered by the descriptivist as having caused the change and no additional inner causality questions are asked. This is perhaps the opposed extreme to the mentality which calculates unending causal connections (cf. §1.). Still, and not in an opposed manner, the dependency concept (cf. also §1.) or, in other words, the fact of individual incompleteness, is in reality seldom accepted and actualized, so that while many a descriptivist synthesizes all the causal relationships peculiar to a given sound change, he simultaneously insists on analyzing them in an effort to discover the ultimate cause. It is clear that all or no causal elements are relevant, that these causal elements must be distinguished by genus and not by value in respect to the changing sound, and that a final cause can only be a complex and not a simple factor.

Since the several main phonemic changes for the Germanic field described in the handbooks give prominence to the conditioned sounds, and in the interest of causation theory, the following tabulations are set up so that the conventionally held conditioning sounds (environments) determine the groupings. The listing is limited to the consonantal conditioners of primary stressed vowels. Where vowels are coconditioners, they also are included; similarly, weaker stressed conditioned vowels are included if they are commonly described as part of the same change.

The defectiveness of a tabulation such as this lies principally in the fact that it depends on secondary evidence, that is, records the descriptions of sound changes which vary in accuracy and detail according to the different handbooks.[8] Whereas one source writes, e.g. rC (r plus consonant), another specifies the particular consonant(s); or one source may consider only the seeming active phase of the change, e.g. u plus following a becomes o, while another in addition renders also the nonactive phase of the same change, u plus following j stays u; or total environment in one account, e.g. e becomes eo between s and lc, is listed in preference to partial in another, e becomes eo before lc; or fourthly, a change may be treated on one time plane, e.g. $á$ becomes $ó$ after w and before following w, or on staggered levels, e.g. $á$ becomes $ǫ$ before following w, and $ǫ$ becomes $ó$ after w. The environmental descriptions have been recorded here in maximum conventional detail, whether now judged relevant or not, since the immediate purpose is not at all to describe the sound changes; it is simply to compile the raw material in such a way as to be able to extract possible environmental tendencies or affinities among the consonantal conditioners.

3. The basic rule applicable to the tabulation is that, unless marked otherwise, all conditioners follow the conditioned sound. Symbols and abbreviations requiring explanation are: C- = conditioner before the conditioned sound; -*C*- = conditioner between two vowels; *C*-*C* = conditioned sound between two consonants; *CC* = geminate consonants; *2C* = consonant group whether geminated or not; *CC(C)* = any two consonants, the second ≠ to the one in parentheses; *C.a* = conditioned sound before *C* and before a noncontiguous *a*, *ǣ*, or *ō*, but not including *a* of *C.a*/*.u*; *C.i* = conditioned sound before *C* and before an incontiguous *ī*, *i*, *j*; *C.o* = conditioned sound after *C* and before a noncontiguous *a*, *o*, *u*; *C.ŏ* = conditioned sound after *C* and before an incontiguous *a*, *ŏ*, *u*; *C*-.*V* = conditioned sound after *C* and before a noncontiguous *V*; *V* in Pre-language = nasalized vowel; *V.* = vowel resulting by a noncontiguously following conditioner; *VV́* = stress shift from first element to second of the diphthong being conditioned; *A* = any short vowel but *i*; *L* = any liquid; *N* = any nasal; *S* = stays or remains; *S.* = stays or remains by a noncontiguously following conditioner; / = and, or; * = reconstruct; *∅* = zero; + = syllable break; # = word break; ´- = primary stressed syllable; `- = weakly stressed syllable; ´-# = primary stressed open monosyllable; ´C# = primary stressed closed monosyllable; `C# = weakly stressed monosyllable; ´-+ = primary stressed open syllable; ´C+ = primary stressed closed syllable; ´-+.e primary stressed open syllable followed by a noncontiguous palatal vowel or vocalic liquid or nasal. The section headings with Pre- include Germanic.

	PRE-GOTHIC		j	j	e > i.
					i > S.
h	h	i > ai			u > S.
		u > au			eu > íu.
hv	hv	i > ai			
			l	l.a	eu > éo.
l	LC	V̄ > V̆		LC	V̄ > V̆
n	Nh	a > ą̄			
		i > ī	**m**	m.a	eu > éo.
		u > ų̄			
	NC	V̄ > V̆	**n**	n.a	eu > éo.
				Nf	a > ą́/ǫ́
r	r	i > ai			i > í/ę́
		u > au			u > ǫ́
				Nh	a > ą́/ǫ́
	PRE-OLD NORSE (P-ON)				i > í/ę́
					u > ǫ́
d	d.a	eu > éo.		Ns	a > ą́/ǫ́
đ	đ.a	eu > éo.			i > í/ę́
					u > ǫ́
h	h	ai > á		NC	e > i
	h.a	i > é.			i > S
		u > ó.			u > S
		ī > é.			V̄ > V̆
		ū > ó.		NC.a	i > é./e.
		au > ó.			u > ó./o.

P-ON (CONT.)

r	r	ai > á
R	R	i > e
		u > o
		ī > é
s	s.a	eu > éo.
w	w	ai > á/ǽ/ey/ei
a	a	i > e.
		u > o.
		eu > éo.
ĭ	ĭ	e > i.
		i > S.
		u > S.
		eu > íu.
ǣ	ǣ	i > e.
		u > o.
		eu > éo.
ō	ō	i > e.
		u > o.
		eu > éo.
u	u	eu > íu.
ꞌ	ꞌ	e > i
	ꞌrA	e > S

ia > æ.
io > ø.
ió > ǿ.
iu > y.
iú > ý.
ua > uæ.
uá > uǽ.

OLD NORSE (ON)

đ	đ	V̆ > V̄
f	fđ	au > ǫ
g	g-	é > je
	gi	a > e
h	h	V̆ > V̄
	h.a/.u	e > S.
	h-	é > je
	h#	ei > é
		au > ó
	hw-	ǫ. > o/S
j	j	a > æ.
		o > ø.
		ǫ. > ø.
		u > y.
		á > ǽ.
		ó > ǿ.
		ǫ. > ǿ.
		ú > ý.
		au > æy.
k	k-	é > je
	ki	a > e
l	l	ǫ. > ó/S
	l-.a/.u	e > S.
	lf	a > á
		o > ó
		ǫ. > ǫ́.
		u > ú
	lg	a > á
		o > ó
		ǫ. > ǫ́.
		u > ú
	lh	V̆ > V̄
	lk	a > á
		o > ó
		ǫ. > ǫ́.
		u > ú
	lm	a > á
		o > ó
		ǫ. > ǫ́.
		u > ú
	lp	a > á
		o > ó
		ǫ. > ǫ́.
		u > ú
m	m	ǫ́. > ó/S
		V̆ > V̄
	m-	ǫ́. > ó/S
n	n	ǫ́. > ó/S
	n-	ǫ́. > ó/S
	ng	a > á
		ǫ. > S
		ei > e
	nk	a > á
		ǫ. > S
	N	ǫ́. > ó
		ea > S
		eo > S
		éa > S
		éo > S
		íu > S

ON (CONT.)

	N-	ǫ̣. > ó.
r	r-.a/.u	e > S.
	rC(h)	ó > o
R	R	a > æ
		o > ø
		o > ó
		ø > ǿ/S
		u > ø
		u > y
		u > ú
		y > ý/S
		á > ǽ
		ó > ǿ
		ú > ý
		au > æy
		iú > ý
s	st	ǫ̣. > ó/S
		ei > e
w	w	a > ǫ.
		æ. > ø.
		e > ø.
		i > y.
		á > ǫ́.
		é > ǿ.
		í > ý.
		ǫ̣. > ó
		ei > ey.
		V̄ > V̆
	w-	á > ó
		ǫ̣. > ó
		ea > S
		eo > S
		éa > S
		éo > S
		íu > S
	w-.u	æ. > ø.
	w-.a/.u	e > S.
	Cw-	a > o
		e > o
z	z#	ei > é
		au > ó
CC	CC(<ht)	V̄ > V̆
a	a	e > ia.
i	ĭ/-ir	a > æ.
		o > ø.

		ǫ̣. > ø.
		u > y.
		á > æ.
		ó > ǿ.
		ǫ̣. > ǿ.
		ú > ý.
		au > æy.
		ia > æ.
		io > ø.
		ió > ǿ.
		iu > y.
		iú > ý.
		ua > uæ.
		uá > uǽ.
u	u	a > ǫ.
		æ. > ø.
		e > ø.
		á > ǫ́.
		ia > iǫ.
		ua > uǫ.
+	+V̆	V̄ > V̆
vv́	vv́	ea > ja
		eo > jo
		éa > já
		éo > jó
		íu > jú

PRE-OLD ENGLISH (P-OE)

b	bb.ð	a > S.
c	c.o	ā > S.
	cc.ð	a > S.
f	ff.ð	a > S.
g	g.o	ā > S.
h	h	a > æ
		ā > ō
		ē > ō
	ht	ō > ð
		ū > ŭ
	hC	ī > ĭ
j	j	e > i.
		i > S.
		u > S.
		eu > īo.
l	LC	V̄ > V̆
m	m	e > i

P-OE (CONT.)

n	N	a > o/S
		u > S
		ā > ō
	Nf	a > ǭ
		i > ī̧
		u > ū̧
	Nh	a > ǭ
		i > ī̧
		u > ū̧
	Ns	a > ǭ
		i > ī̧
		u > ū̧
	N⫯	a > ǭ
		i > ī̧
		u > ū̧
	NC	e > i
		i > S
		u > S
		Ṽ > V̄
p	p.o	ā > S.
	pp.ŏ	a > S.
r	r.o	ā > S.
s	sc.ŏ	a > S.
	ss.ŏ	a > S.
	st.ŏ	a > S.
t	tt.ŏ	a > S.
w	w	a > S
	w.o	ā > S.
	wV	e > eo
	w#	au > ēa
		eu > ēo
a	a	i > e.
		u > o.
		eu > ēo.
ĭ	ĭ	e > i.
		i > S.
		u > S.
		eu > īo.
æ̆	ǣ	i > e.
		u > o.
		eu > ēo.
ð	ō	i > e.
		u > o.
		eu > ēo.
u	u	eu > īo.

‘C+	‘C+	a > æ
‘+	‘+.e	a > æ.
	‘+.o	a > S.
-	‘	e > i
	‘rA	e > S

OLD ENGLISH (OE)

b	b-cc	o > u
c	·c	y. > i
		ȳ. > ī
		ea > e/S
		ie > i
		īe > ī
	·c-	æ > ea
		e > ie
		y > i
		ǣ > ēa
		ea > e/S
		ēa > ē/S
	c.o	æ > S.
		e > S.
		i > S.
	cg	y. > i
		ȳ. > ī
	c⫯	y. > i
		ȳ. > ī
d	d.o	æ > ea./S.
		e > eo./S.
		i > io./S.
đ	đ.o	æ > ea./S.
		e > eo./S.
		i > io./S.
f	f.o	æ > ea.
		e > eo.
		i > io.
	fhV	i > ī
	f-g	o > u
	f-l	o > u
g	·g	y. > i
		ȳ. > ī
		ēa > ē/S
		ie > i
		īe > ī
	·g-	æ > ea
		e > ᶖie
		o > ęo

OE (CONT.)

	context	rule
		u > i̯u
		ā > ęā
		ǣ > ēa
		ē > īe
		ō > ęō
		ū > i̯ū
		ea > e/S
		ēa > ē/S
	·gd	æ > ǣ
		e > ē
		i > ī
	·gđ	æ > ǣ
		e > ē
		i > ī
	·gn	æ > ǣ
		e > ē
		i > ī
	·gs	æ > ǣ
		e > ē
		i > ī
	-g-	ige > ī
		igi > ī
	g.o	æ > S
		e > S
		i > S
h	h	æ > ea
		e > eo
		o > ō/S
		ǣ > ēa
		ē > ēo
		ī > īo
		y > i
		ea > e/S
		ēa > ē/S
		ie > i
		īe > ī
		V̆ > V̄
	hg	ēa > ē/S
	hs	ēa > ē/S
		eo > ie/i/y
	ht	ęa > ie/i/y
		eo > ie/i/y
		ō > ŏ
		ū > ŭ
	h⸜	ēa > ē/S
	hC(j)	æ > ea
		e > eo
		i > io
	-h-	V̆ > V̄

letter	context	rule
j	j	a > e.
		æ > e.
		o > e.
		u > y.
		ā > ǣ.
		ō > ē.
		ū > ȳ.
		ea > ie.
		ēa > īe.
		io > ie.
		īo > īe.
	jh	i > ī
l	l.o	æ > ea
		e > eo
		i > io
	lc	e > eo
	ld	V̆ > V̄
	l-f	o > u
	lh	e > eo
		i > io
	lhV	u > ū
		ea > ēa
		eo > ēo
	lC(j)	æ > ea/a
m	mb	V̆ > V̄
n	n·c	y. > i
		ȳ. > ī
	nd	V̆ > V̄
	nhV	o > ō
	N.o	æ > ea./S.
		e > eo./S.
		i > io./S.
p	p.o	æ > ea.
		e > eo.
		i > io.
r	r.o	æ > ea.
		e > eo.
		i > io.
	rd	V̆ > V̄
	rhV	*o > ō
		u > ū
		y. > ȳ
		ea > ēa
		eo > ēo
	rn	V̆ > V̄
	rC(j)	æ > ea
		e > eo

OE (CONT.)

		i > io
s	s	ie > i
		īe > ī
	sc	a > ęa
		æ > ea
		e > ie
	e. > ie
		o > ęo
		u > įu
		ā > ęā
		ǣ > ēa
		ǣ. > ēa
		ē. > *īe
		ō > ęō
		ū > įū
		ea > e/S
		ēa > ē/S
	s.o	æ > ea.
		e > eo.
		i > io.
	s-lf	e > eo
	s-lh	e > eo
t	t.o	æ > ea./S.
		e > eo./S.
		i > io./S.
w	w	a > ea
		e > eo
		e. > eo
		i > io
		ā > ēa/S
		ǣ > ēa/S
		ǣ. > ēa/S
		ī > īo/S
	w-	i > y/S
		ie > y/S
		io > u
	w-l	o > u
	w-r	eo > o/u/y
	w-s	eo > o
	w-st	eo > o/u/y
	w-t	eo > u
CC	CC	V̄ > V̆
	2C.i	æ > S.
	2C.o	æ > S.
		e > S.
		i > S.
ĭ	ĭ	a > e.

æ > e.
o > e.
u > y.
ā > ǣ.
ō > ē.
ū > ȳ.
ea > ie.
ēa > īe.
io > ie.
īo > īe.

´⚹	´#	V̄ > V̆

PRE-OLD SAXON (P-OS)

g	g-	ā > ē
j	j	e > i.
		i > S.
		u > S.
		ai > ęi.
		eu > iu./eo.
k	k-	ā > ē
l	LC	V̄ > V̆
m	m	e > i
		ā > ō/ū/S
n	N	o > u/S
		u > S
		ā > ō/ū/S
	Nf	a > ą̈/ǫ
		i > į̄
		u > ų
	Nh	a > ą̈/ǫ
		i > į̄
		u > ų̄
	N⸽	a > ą̈/ǫ
		i > į̄
		u > ų̄
	NC	e > i
		i > S
		u > S
		V̄ > V̆
w	w	au > S
		e > i
	w.a	eu > S.
a	a	i > e./S.
		u > o.
		eu > eo.

	P-OS (CONT.)			h-r	o > u
ĭ	ĭ	e > i.	j	j	a > e.
		i > S.			o > ö.
		u > S.			u > i.
		ai > ẹi.			ā > ē.
		eu > eo./iu.			ō > ē.
u	u	e > i.			ū > ī.
		eu > eo./iu.			uo > ue.
ǣ	ǣ	i > e./S.		j-k	o > u
		u > o.	k	k	o > u/S
		eu > eo.		·k	a > e/S
ō	ō	i > e./S.			ā > ē/S
		u > o.		k-m	o > u
		eu > eo.	l	l	e > a/S
ᴧ	ᴧ	e > i			o > a/S
	ᴧrA	e > S.			ēo > eo
ᴧ※	ᴧ#	eu > S		ld	a > o/S
					ē > e
	OLD SAXON (OS)			ld.i	a > ä.
				ll	ē > e
b	bd.i	a > ä.		lt	a > o/S
d	.d	o > a/S.		l-f	o > u
f	f	o > a/S		ᴧlC	a > o
	f-g	o > u	m	m-l	o > u
	f-l	o > u	n	n	a > o/S
g	·g	a > e/S			e > i/S
		e > i/S			e. > i/S
		ā > ē/S			o > u/S
	·g-	e > i/S			ā > ō/S
		ā > ē/S		nd.i	a > ä.
	-g-	agi > ei		ng	ē > e
		egi > ei		nC	a > o/S
		igi > ī		nC.i	a > ä.
	g-m	o > u		n-m	o > u
h	h	a > o/S	p	p	o > u
		i > iu/S		p-r	o > u
		u > o/S	r	r	a > e/S
		V̆ > Ṽ			a > o/S
	-h-	aha > ā			e > a/S
		eho > ē			e > i/S
	hl.i	a > ä.			e. > i/S
	hn.i	a > ä.			i > e/S
	hs.i	a > ä.			o > a/S
	ht	Ṽ > Ṽ			u > o/S
	ht.i	a > ä.		rb.i	a > ä.
	hw-	uo > o		rd.i	a > ä.
				rg.i	a > ä.

OS (CONT.)

					u > S	
	rn.i	a > ä.			V̆ > V̆	
	rw.i	a > ä.	r	r.a	eu > eo.	
	r-m	o > u		rC.a	i > e.	
s	s	e > o/u/S	s	s.a	i > e.	
	sw-	uo > o			eu > eo.	
	s-m	o > u		ss.a	i > e.	
	s-C	we > u	t	t.a	eu > eo.	
t	tr	ē > e	w	w	e > i/S	
		ū > u		ww	e > i	
w	w	V̆ > V̆		w.a	eu > S.	
	w-	a > o/S	z	z.a	eu > eo.	
		e > o/S	a	a	i > e.	
		i > u/S			u > o.	
		uo > o			eu > eo.	
	w-l	i > Ø	ĭ	ĭ	e > i.	
		o > u			i > S.	
	w-n	i > Ø			u > S.	
	w-r	a > o			eu > iu.	
	-w-	iwi > ī	u	u	e > i.	
ĭ	ĭ	a > e.			eu > iu.	
		o > ö.	æ	ǣ	i > e.	
		u > i.			u > o.	
					eu > eo.	
ʾ	ʾ	a > o/S	ō	ō	i > e.	
	ʾ̆	a > ä.			u > o.	
					eu > eo.	
ʾ#	ʾ#	e > ē/ie/S	ʾ	ʾ	e > i	
		u > ū/S		ʾrA	e > S.	

PRE-OLD HIGH GERMAN (P-OHG)

d	d.a	eu > eo.
h	h.a	eu > eo.
j	j	e > i.
		i > S.
		u > S.
		eu > iu.
l	l.a	eu > eo.
	LC	V̆ > V̆
m	m.a	u > o./S.
n	n.a	eu > eo.
	Nh	a > ą̄
		i > į̄
		u > ų̄
	NC	e > i
		i > S

OLD HIGH GERMAN (OHG)

ch	ch.i	a > ä.
	ch-m	a > o/S
d	d	ai > ē/S
f	f-l	a > o/S
g	g	e > ie/S
		i > ie/S
	-g-	egi > ei
h	h	e > io/eo/S
		i > ie/S
		u > o/S
		u > uo/S
		ē > eo/S

OHG (CONT.)					
			n	n	ai > ē/S
		ī > ie/S			au > ō
		ī > i/S	**r**	r	i > ie/S
		ō > o/S			ai > ē
		ū > uo/S			au > ō
		ai > ē		rC.i	a > ä.
		au > ō			
		ie > i/S	**s**	s	au > ō
		uo > u/S			
	h.i	a > ä.	**t**	t	au > ō
	hh.i	a > ä.			
	hs.i	a > ä.	**w**	w	ai > ē
	ht.i	a > ä.		w-	e > o/S
	-h-	V̆hV̄ > V̄			i > u/S
	ꞌh#	a > o			o > e/S
		e > o			u > S
				w-m	a > o
j	j	a > e.	**z**	z	au > ō
		o > ö.			
		u > ü.	**C**	Cw.i	a > ä.
		ā > æ.	**ĭ**	ĭ	a > e.
		ō > ö.			o > ö.
		ū > ü.			u > ü.
		ou > öu.			ā > æ.
		uo > üe.			ō > ö.
	-j-	ijō > iu			ū > ü.
		uji > iu/ui			ou > öu.
					uo > üe.
1	1	a > o/S			
		au > ō	ꞌ	ꞌĭ	a > ä.
	1C.i	a > ä.			
m	m-h	a > o/S	ꞌ*	#	ai > ē/S
	m-n	a > o/S			au > ō

4. Prokosch noted a definite patterning among the Germanic consonantal conditioners:

> There is a great consistency in the degree to which different consonants influence vowels. Arranged in accordance with this, the active consonants are: *ɦ r l, dentals*; *w* exerts similar influences, but can hardly be assigned a definite place within this scale. The form of influence varies considerably in the several dialects, but the general agreement is too significant to be considered accidental. The effect of these consonants consists essentially in a lowering and backing of the articulation of the preceding vowel.[9]

The above statement is an indication of the potential of the collective consonantal conditioners. Other descriptive statements can be found scattered in various treatments of individual sound changes; while they yield some information as to one (or more conditioners), they do not attempt to say anything definitive about the conditioner as belonging to a class of conditioners, whether in one language or in a diasystem.[10]

From the tabulation in §3, it appears that there may well be others than Prokosch's five plus nasals 'active' categories (cf. note 9) especially if affinities with the various umlauting types are established and in particular with consonantal *i* and *u*. For example, Holtzmann's Law, which formulates a common origin for a vowel-consonant split, and the syllabics themselves suggest a possible minimum distinction between vowels and consonants. In changes where a certain degree of stress or a type of juncture is a coconditioner with either a vowel and/or consonant, the gap between suprasegmental and segmental appears narrowed.[11]

The listings of the sound changes present the raw material in only one dimension and by means of conventional orthography. Although the kind of modification in the conditioned sound can, in part at least, be recognized by this representation, neither the phonetic nor phonemic state of the conditioner is indicated. Reference-book descriptions frequently touch upon the 'fate' of the conditioner secondarily, as e.g. 'lost' in the case of a vowel lengthened in compensation, or 'weakened' by being partially assimilated into a preceding vowel; these were entirely excluded since it is conjectured that traditional statements about conditioners are inadequate generally and often particularly.

To fully interpret the evidence, the listings could be rearranged so as to be viewed from many angles, and for comparative purposes, several other directions of descriptive approach might be undertaken and drawn in, e.g. tabulation of vocalic conditioners in consonant changes; consonantal conditioners in consonant changes; junctural conditioners; changes in weaker stressed syllables, including the behavior and nature of phonemes under Auslautsgesetze; a thorough study of phenomena like ecthlipsis and epenthesis, which involve precisely many of the 'consonantal conditioners'; and a reevaluation of so-called 'exceptions' to sound laws.

In conclusion, it is probably not unreasonable to venture a phonetic-phonemic statement concerning the overall picture of the early Germanic consonantal conditioners of stressed vowels: similar to laryngeal conditioners, but by no means to be equated with them en masse, the consonantal conditioners do not possess purely consonantal features, but they possess vocalic features as well.

NOTES

1   *Word* 19.324, 323 (1963).
2   F. de Saussure, *Course in general linguistics*, W. Baskin, trans.; C. Bally et al., eds. (New York, 1959), says: 'We must draw up for each language studied a

phonological system, i.e. a description of the sounds with which it functions; for each language operates on a fixed number of well-differentiated phonemes ... [p. 34]   Any language operates with a clearly delimited gamut of phonemes' [p. 221].

3   J. Kurylowicz, 'On the methods of internal reconstruction', *Proceedings of the ninth international congress of linguists,* M. Halle, ed., 11 (The Hague, 1964), writes: 'Physiological speculations, such as the increased intensity of articulation, "prononciation à glotte ouverte" ..., do not grasp the *linguistic* essence of these changes, the shift of the *internal* relations of the elements in question being the only pertinent fact. The external stimuli of the changes are extrinsic to the phonemic system. Once we leave language *sensu stricto* and appeal to extralinguistic factors, a clear delimitation of the field of linguistic research is lost.'

4   'The biological model and historical linguistics', *Language* 39.169 (1963). A well-described instance of the functioning of ordered chance is to be seen in W. P. Lehmann's realia-founded explication of 'Some phonological observations based on examination of the Germanic consonant shift', *Monatshefte* 60.234 (1963) where the 'selection and chance variation mechanism' is reflected in the term 'differential indicator'. Lehmann writes that 'the fundamental variable unit in the evolution of language is the differential indicator, not the phoneme'; and in identifying the differential indicator as he does for the Consonant Shift, a concrete example is had.

5   'If there is one thing that has been clearly brought out by the latest advances in physics, it is that in our experience there are different "spheres" or "levels" in the unity of nature, each of them distinguished by the dominance of certain factors which are imperceptible or negligible in a neighboring sphere or on an adjacent level' (Teilhard de Chardin, *The phenomenon of man,* Bernard Wall, trans., 54 [New York, 1960]).

6   Ibid. 44–5: 'In its different orders of magnitude, matter never repeats its different combinations ... These multiple zones of the cosmos envelop without imitating each other in such a way that we cannot pass from one to another by a simple change of coefficients. Here is no repetition of the same theme on a different scale. The order and design do not appear except in the whole.'

7   H. M. Hoenigswald, *Language change and linguistic reconstruction* 75 (Chicago, 1960), always conveys this concept in terms of 'replacement' which in itself presupposes a setting: 'The replacement pattern of sound change—as distinct from its physical content—is the crucial factor in structural phonological change; by the same token, its analysis provides the tools for phonologic reconstruction.'

8   Those mainly followed were: W. Braune, *Althochdeutsche Grammatik*[11] (Tübingen, 1963); W. Braune, *Gotische Grammatik*[16] (Tübingen, 1961); F. Dieter, ed. *Laut- und Formenlehre der Altgermanischen Dialekte* (Leipzig, 1900); H. Gallée, *Altsächsische Grammatik*[2] (Halle, 1910); E. V. Gordon, *An introduction to Old Norse*[2] (Oxford, 1957); H. Hirt, *Handbuch des Urgermanischen* vol. 1, *Laut- und Akzentlehre* (Heidelberg, 1931); F. Holthausen, *Altsächsisches Elementarbuch*[2] (Heidelberg, 1921); A. Lasch, *Mittelniederdeutsche Grammatik*

(Halle, 1914); S. Moore and T. A. Knott, *The elements of Old English*[10] (Ann Arbor, Mich., 1955); A. Noreen, *Altisländische und Altnorwegische Grammatik*[2] (Halle, 1892); E. Prokosch, *A comparative Germanic grammar* (Philadelphia, 1939); J. Schatz, *Althochdeutsche Grammatik* (Göttingen, 1927); E. Sievers and K. Brunner, *Altenglische Grammatik*[2] (Halle/Saale, 1942); J. Wright, *Grammar of the Gothic language*[2] (Oxford, 1954); J. Wright, *Old English grammar*[2] (Oxford, 1914).

9 Prokosch 114; on p. 113 he considers the *nasals* as conditioners.

10 However, H. Penzl in his 'Old High German ⟨r⟩ and its phonetic identification', *Lg.* 37.488–96 (1961), extracts some of the evidence for the features of OHG /r/ from its function as a shared conditioner in several OHG sound changes.

11 A. Martinet, *Elements of general linguistics*, E. Palmer, trans., 190 (London, 1960), in dealing with cause seems convinced about general suprasegmental effect: '... in the final analysis the elements of disequilibrium result from the changing needs of the speakers of a language; ... it is probably through the agency of prosodic facts, like the accent, that needs of communication have their most direct repercussions on phonological systems.'

7

A PRELIMINARY DESIGN FOR
AN ANALYTIC GRAMMAR OF SANSKRIT

Richard H. Robinson

1. THE PROBLEM. The usual grammar of Sanskrit is synthetic rather than analytic; it states how the constituents are to be combined into constitutes rather than how constitutes are to be resolved into constituents; it lays out a grid of categories and then gives instructions for filling in the blank paradigm; it does not give instructions for finding the right slot in the paradigm to which a given form belongs. Thus, the existing grammars are for writers rather than readers of Sanskrit, even though most people who consult a Sanskrit grammar wish to read rather than to compose.

Everyone who has learned to read Sanskrit has by some means or other acquired an analytic grammar. He has learned to resolve sandhi forms, to identify word boundaries, to recognize the gender, case, number, tense, voice, and person of inflected words, and to understand syntactic relations. In short, he has learned to move from the page to the paradigm. This is such a protracted and highly frustrating process that the majority of students give up during the elementary phase. It is true that Lanman's *Reader*[1] provides in its notes copious references to the paradigms, but it does not tell the student how to proceed if he has to identify a form for himself. The teacher consequently finds himself formulating ad hoc analytic rules to satisfy the students' recurrent question: 'How can you tell what this form is?'

The pedagogical need for an analytic grammar is evident. The purely linguistic interest lies in the grammatical design. Georg von der Gabelentz discussed the distinction between writers' and readers' grammars in 1878.[2] But the recent trend has, under the influence of algebraic models, become even more exclusively concerned with constructing forms, to the neglect of the diagnostic, identifying function.

This article is a preliminary exploration of the methodology for setting up an analytic grammar. I intend in due course to produce such a grammar, and then this present exercise will no doubt have some retrospective interest. The objective of the grammar is to provide a set of formal rules and lists such that someone ignorant of Sanskrit can identify all the grammatical phenomena on a page of text written in Devanāgarī script. The grammar is to be written primarily for human use, but might also be

adapted for machine use so that lengthy texts could be analyzed gram
matically by computer.

An analytic grammar is a statement for a language that has already been
analyzed, and is not a set of procedures for analyzing Sanskrit as if it were
an unknown language. The methodology is one of description rather than
of discovery. The ordinary synthetic grammar is in fact written by first
analyzing the language and then reversing the process so that the description states how to synthesize.

It is assumed that everyone who can read Sanskrit has at his command
an analytic grammar of the language. But it need not be assumed that all
readers operate with the same set of informal rules and procedures. Further,
the language is sufficiently redundant and there are enough alternative
markers, so that the same grammatical fact can often be recognized in more
than one way. An ideal analytic grammar would be based on a complete
inventory of grammatical signals, statistics of their frequency in a sizable
corpus, and calculations of the relative utility of the signals that participate
in redundancies. I do not propose to write an ideal grammar, so the following discussion of method is directed toward a formalization of my own
Sanskrit reading operations insofar as I am able to bring them to conscious
notice.

2. WHAT IS GIVEN. It is assumed that the Devanāgarī orthography is
given, and that the user of the grammar has learned to recognize all the
letters and combinations of letters. The standard tables of Devanāgarī
letters and their roman-letter equivalents belong equally to the synthetic
and the analytic grammar. All the reader need do is to read the table in
the opposite direction from that in which the writer reads it.

Also taken as given are:

1. The lexicon—the list of declinable stems, invariant words, and verb
   roots together with their meanings. This includes some grammatical information such as the gender of nouns, the principal
   and irregular parts of verbs, and the cases that certain lexemes
   select. For present purposes 'lexicon' shall mean Monier-Williams'
   Sanskrit-English dictionary.[3]

2. The paradigms of declension and conjugation. For present purposes
   this means the paradigms in Whitney's *Sanskrit grammar* and the
   paradigmatic information in his *Roots, verb-forms, and primary
   derivatives*.[4]

3. The syntactic rules of Classical Sanskrit. Whitney's statements on
   syntax, supplemented by information in the lexicon, though by
   no means complete or lucid, are adequate for the present paper.

4. The morphophonemic (sandhi) rules of Classical Sanskrit. These are

stated quite fully and rather obscurely by Whitney, clearly and less fully by Emeneau.[5]

5. The usual morphological analysis of the inflectional paradigms. This yields: (a) a list of inflectional endings, (b) a list of thematic suffixes, (c) the augment, (d) vowel gradation (guṇa and vṛddhi) of the verb root, and (e) reduplication of the verb root.
6. Whatever elements of the derivational morphology are diagnostic for inflectional morphology. This includes the verbal prefixes (preverbs), the invariant verbal suffixes (infinitive and gerunds), and a list of suffixes that form declinable stems. The membership of the last list cannot be established prior to writing the grammar, so the preliminary list must be inclusive.

The Devanāgarī orthography indicates some but not all word boundaries. On a page chosen at random (Lanman 1883.47) there are 147 boundaries, of which the orthography indicates only 117, leaving 30 to be inferred. It would be possible and much easier to base an analytic grammar on romanized Sanskrit in which words are separated by spaces, and compounds divided by hyphens. But it is more useful and more interesting to follow the more difficult alternative and take word boundaries only where the Devanāgarī indicates them.

3. ANALYTIC OPERATIONS. The operations for which the analytic grammar must provide are:

(a) segmentation of word from word;
(b) conversion of word-final sandhi forms to in pausa form;
(c) segmentation of case-number endings from declined stems;
(d) segmentation of person-number endings from conjugated stems;
(e) segmentation of verb theme-suffixes (including infinitive, gerund, and participles) from roots;
(f) segmentation of the augment from verb stems and verb prefixes;
(g) identification of the root underlying reduplication and vowel gradation;
(h) identification of lexemes in the lexicon;
(i) location of affixes in the paradigms of the stems to which they are attached, and identification of the grammatical categories—gender, case, number; tense-mood, voice, person—of which they are the exponents;
(j) segmentation and interpretation of compounds;
(k) identification of syntactic relations from the morphological expressions of agreement and government and from function words such as the enclitics.

It is not possible to order these operations in such a way that each can

KEY TO PARSING CODE

Order of symbols for declension: gender, case, number.
Order of symbols for conjugation: tense-mood, voice, person, number.

GENDER		NUMBER		VOICE	
m	masculine	s	singular	a	active
f	feminine	d	dual	m	middle
n	neuter	p	plural	p	passive

CASE		TENSE-MOOD		INVARIANTS	
N	nominative	P	present indicative	a	adverb
A	accusative	M	imperfect	e	enclitic
I	instrumental	I	imperative	p	preposition
D	dative	O	optative	c	conjunction
B	ablative	E	perfect	i	infinitive
G	genitive	A	aorist	g	gerund
L	locative	F	future		
V	vocative	C	conditional		

be completed before the next is begun. When the orthography segments the words, the analyst can proceed immediately to resolve the sandhi. But when it does not, he must proceed to another operation, leaving the word divisions to be effected later. Which operation should normally be applied first in such cases? Apart from the augment and reduplication, the grammatical extensions are suffixed rather than prefixed to lexemes. So the analyst may either look up the lexemes and identify word-beginnings, or look up the endings and identify the word finals. But sandhi applies principally to word finals. Consequently, fewer variants have to be normalized to look up the lexemes than to look up the endings (see §4.1 for treatment of endings in the morphological list). Furthermore, many endings cannot be identified until the shape of the stem is known. For example, in the code -*o* may be:

a) a sandhi variant of -*as*, which is
   i. mNs of stems in *a*- (*devas*),
   ii. BGs and Ap of consonant stems when added to weak stem (*rājñas*), and NVp when added to strong stem (*rājānas*),
   iii. nNAs of derivative nouns in *as*- with zero ending (*manas*),
   iv. Ma2s of thematic verbs (*abhavas, apaśyas*),
   v. Aa2s of certain verbs (*asicas, amūmucas, adikṣas*),

vi. Ca2s (*abhaviṣyas*), or

b) sandhi-normal *-o*, Vs of stems in *u-* (*sātro, dheno, madho*).

Operations (f) and (g) must be performed before the lexeme can be located. Since the augment is a single morpheme with two allomorphs (*a-* before consonants, and vṛddhi of vowel initials) one should suspect all initial *a*'s and vṛddhis of being augments until the lexicon and the morphology show them to be or not to be. Reduplication is easily recognized and the root can be readily recovered.

A vowel grade of roots cannot be correctly interpreted without the assistance of morphology. Often derivational suffixes mark a stem as a declinable and so eliminate the possibility that the lexeme is a verb root either with or without the guṇa that the occurrent form exhibits. (*bhavana* is marked as a declinable by *-ana-*, so there is no reason to suspect it of belonging to the paradigm of the verb *bhū*.) The causative suffix *-aya-* selects the guṇa of medial, and the vṛddhi of final, high vowels. Thus, its presence is a signal to reduce the vowel grade in order to find the underlying lexeme, a verb root. The case of denominatives which have the same suffix *-aya-* (*arthaya-*, *ākarṇaya-*) can be handled by providing in the rules that the analyst shall look in the lexicon for a stem containing *-aya-* and shall not proceed to drop the suffix and downgrade the vowel unless he fails to find the lexeme by the first procedure. Other rules for downgrading the vowel before looking in the lexicon may be formulated with thematic suffixes and personal endings as the occurrents that invoke the rule. The Pa1s, 2s, and 3s endings *-mi, -si,* and *-ti*, for instance, coming after a monosyllable with guṇa vowel, are signals to downgrade and discover a root as the underlying lexeme—*dveṣmi, dvekṣi,* and *dveṣṭi* from root *dviṣ*.

The last example is illustrative of cases where the endings are more readily identified than the lexemes. Some endings are subject to no sandhi changes, or only to the most transparent ones—*-bhyah* and *-bhyo* from *-bhyas* DBp; *-ṣu, -ṣv,* and *-sv* from *-su* Lp; *-oḥ* and *-or* from *-os* GLd. Many endings are quite unlikely to be confused with false segments, and so can be identified with ease at any stage of the analysis—*-bhyam* IDBd, *-mahe* Pm1p and Em1p, *-mahai* Im1p, *-mahi* Mm1p. The analytic grammar ought to contain a list of easily identifiable suffixes and endings keyed to the rules, so that operations (c), (d), and (e) may be begun as soon as possible. Ambiguous endings will then be left until the lexicon and the syntax provide criteria for eliminating wrong identifications.

Operation (e)—segmentation of verb theme-suffixes—usually cannot be performed until it is known that the word is a verb and sometimes must wait until the root has been identified in the lexicon, since the conjugation class of a root often decides which of two homophonous affixes the occurrent is. *jāyate* 'be born' is Pm3s of root *jā* with class-4 present stem suffix *-ya-*. *jñāyate* 'be known' is Pp3s of the class-9 root *jñā*, with passive suffix *-ya-*. If *-ya-* is followed by an active ending (*paśyati* 'he sees') the form is clearly a class-4 present stem. But if the ending is middle (*jāyate*) the ambivalence of the form cannot be resolved by mere inspection.

When all the straightforward analytic operations have been performed, there remains a residue of unidentified word boundaries, unresolved sandhi, and endings that are either unidentified or have more than one possible identification. Most of these are instances where old-fashioned authorities say that one 'has to tell from the context', without giving instructions for doing so. It is possible and advantageous to make these operations explicit. Semantic congruence is one of the criteria; the alternative that makes sense is more likely to be the right one. Grammatical congruence is at least as important a criterion; when one form has two grammatical identities, the one that is in agreement or government with a nearby form is the more likely identification. In *gate pitari*, for example, *gate* may be:

> i. EpmLs of *gata* 'gone',
> ii. EpnLs of *gata* 'gone',
> iii. nNAVd of *gata*, 'gone',
> iv. fVs of *gatā* 'gone',
> v. fNAVd of *gatā* 'gone',
> vi. fVs of *gati* 'a course, a going'.

But *pitari* is unambiguously mLs. Therefore *gate* is mLs. The locative absolute pattern (a participle and a noun agreeing in gender and number, and both in the locative [Whitney, 1889.303c, d]) is quite frequent, a fact that reinforces the identification.

The reckoning of transitional probabilities is complicated by the fact that order is only marginally significant and discontinuities are commonplace in Sanskrit syntax. Nevertheless proximity is a strong indication that if the morphology does not exclude the possibility then the two words are in agreement or government. An ideal grammar would contain a tabulation of the probabilities calculated from samples of texts in the major styles of both verse and prose. A nonideal grammar can at least record and organize the incidental observations of readers and teachers of Sanskrit.

> *teṣāṃ tadā nivasatāṃ satāṃ kālas tapasyatām aticakrāma.*
> (*Mahābhārata*, Tale of Sāvitrī, 11.186–7)

nivasatām may be: (i) Ia3d, (ii) Im3s, (iii) PamGp, or (iv) PanGp of *ni-vas* 'dwell'. Similarly for *tapasyatām* from *tapasya* 'practice austerity'. But *teṣām* is Gp so, notwithstanding the intervening *tadā*, *nivasatām* is more likely to be Gp than anything else. *kālas* is mNs and in agreement with the

Ea3s verb *aticakrāma*, hence it is improbable that the same sentence contains a string of dual imperatives, and almost as improbable that it contains a string of Im3s.

Conversion of word-final sandhi forms to paradigmatic norms [operation(b)] is possible in many instances before any lexical or morphological identifications have been made. Phonological shape and determining features are sufficient for the operation. For instance, *-ir*, *-īr*, *-ur*, *-ūr*, *-er*, *-or*, *-air*, *-aur* before a sonant initial and *-iḥ*, *-īḥ*, *-uḥ*, *-ūḥ*, *-eḥ*, *-oḥ*, *-aiḥ*, *-auḥ* before a surd (including pause) represent paradigmatic *-is*, *-īs*, *-us*, *-ūs*, *-es*, *-os*, *-ais*, *-aus* (excepting a few root-nouns with final *r* such as *gir* 'voice'). The grammar ought to distinguish those sandhi resolutions which are independent of morphology and lexicon from those which are dependent. The rules ought to be related to a list of shapes that can occur word-final, and should provide instructions on how to proceed in either case.

4. STRUCTURE AND CONTENTS OF THE ANALYTIC GRAMMAR

4.1. THE LISTS. Of the things taken as given (in §3), only the lexicon and the alphabet are appropriately organized. The statements of sandhi, morphology, and syntax must all be rewritten in a suitable form and ordered for reference purposes. It is obvious that there should be three lists, no more and no less: sandhi, morphology, and syntax. But many facts could be assigned to either or both of two lists, and the choice requires justification. The criteria are: (a) convenience for reference, (b) economy of statement, (c) clarity of statement. But (a) and (b) are often in conflict; the fuller the list, the fewer times the reader has to refer or cross-refer, but the smaller the economy of statement. Likewise, (b) and (c) may come into conflict. The decision here depends on the purpose of the grammar. If it is to be memorized by the reader, then economy takes some precedence over convenience and clarity. If it is to be used for reference, economy is rather unimportant. At this point it seems reasonable that the grammar should consist of two parts: the lists of forms (see §4.1), which ought to be alphabetically arranged and should contain every item of any utility whatsoever; and the rules (see §4.2), which the reader ought to know by heart, and which consequently ought to be stated as economically as completeness and adequate clarity permit.

It is possible to include in the morphology list all sandhi variants of endings with their phonological environments and cross-references to the paradigmatic forms. Thus, *-o* (+ sonant), *-aḥ* (+ surd), *-as* (+ *t-*) might all be listed, with the note that *-as* is the paradigmatic form. But this ending possesses several morphological identities. Listing all of them under each sandhi variant would inflate the list considerably. In addition, *-o* represents paradigmatic *-o* as well as *-as*. The grammarian can count the number of reference operations needed to look first in the sandhi list and then in the morphology list, and compare it with the increased memory burden of the inflated list. But the statistical calculation of net economy is too intricate for my nonideal grammar, and probably would not result in substantially greater convenience.

The sandhi list should be short enough and appropriately arranged to be memorized. The left side of each statement is the occurrent form. The right side lists the resolutions of the occurrent form and the environments of each alternative resolution. The material should be ordered alphabetically so that those who have not memorized the list can operate with it conveniently. External and internal sandhi should be integrated in the same list, the fact that a sandhi is external or internal or both being noted in the statement of its environments. This enables the analyst, when trying to mark word boundaries, to look in only one list to find whether a sandhi form indicates a word final. There is considerable economy and visual clarity to be gained by using notation and tabulation for sandhi statements, but a rhetorical statement is easier to memorize. The grammar should contain both a notational and a rhetorical version of the sandhi list.

The morphology list should certainly contain all declensional and conjugational endings, all forms from the paradigms of the personal and demonstrative pronouns (which are so irregular that there is no practical point in distinguishing stems from endings), and all combinations of stem suffix and ending in the verb system. These latter comprise combinations of participial stem-suffix and case-number endings, as well as of tense-mood signs and person-number endings. The point of segmentation should be between the root and the first suffix, and the list should indicate whether the termination occurs with a weak or strong root, with reduplication, or with augment.

It may be asked whether the list should contain false segmentations as well as true segments. I think that it should not. False segments are not legitimate memory items. They are probably at least as numerous as true segments (this point could be checked by counting a sample), and would inflate the list enormously. The mere fact of their not occurring in the list is a tacit instruction to try another segmentation, and so obviates including them at all. But the inclusion of combinations of suffix and ending eliminates numerous occasions for wrong segmentation. One of the rules should state: when in doubt, segment at what appears to be the end of the root, and look up the right-hand segment.

Example:
  prāpnoti 'he takes'
  segment: *pra-āp-no-ti*

list: *pra*—prefix, 'forward' (lexicon and morphology)

āp—root, 'take' class 5 (lexicon)

no—tense-sign, present stem of class-5 verbs, occurs before Pa1, 2, 3s; Ma2s, 3s, Ia3s

ti—ending, Pa3s, Fa3s, occurs after strong stem

prāp-pra-āp—compound verb, 'take' (lexicon)

noti—Pa3s of class-5 verbs.

It is not necessary to include *pra* in the morphology as it is in the lexicon, but for convenience it and the other preverbs might as well be included. Roots (such as *āp*) are too numerous to warrant duplicating in the lexicon. So the morphology list will contain *pra-, no-, -ti*, and *-noti*.

Whether the morphology should list simple verb stems is worth considering. The stem *āp* has: present *āpnu, āpno*; perfect *āp*; aorist *āp*; and future *āpsya*. All this information is given in the lexicon (Monier-Williams 1872.142a), and is readily located because the root remains undisguised throughout. But *kṛ* 'do' has the stems: present *kuru, karo, kur*; perfect *cakṛ, cakar, cakār*; aorist *(a)kṛṣ, (a)kārṣ*; future *kariṣya*. In all of these, the root is to some extent disguised. A sound general principle is to include in the morphology all stems that, because the root is drastically modified, would be hard to locate in the lexicon. Guṇa would not be considered a drastic modification, so *dveṣ-*, the strong present stem of *dviṣ* 'hate', would not be listed. But reduplications of all kinds, whether for perfect, desiderative, aorist, or present, would qualify for listing. Future stems would ordinarily not need to be included, except when they involve reverse guṇa (*drakṣya-* from *dṛś* 'see').

The European-style Sanskrit grammar presents syntax as if for the reader's sake rather than the writer's, after having presented a morphology for the writer. The usual rubric is 'The uses of ...' Surely no writer is going to deliberate: 'Now that I know how to make locatives, how can I use them?' His question is rather: 'Which case does this verb or adjective govern?' Nevertheless, the syntactic information in Whitney is grouped topically and appended to the various morphology sections, so that even as a grammar for the reader it is inconvenient.

Sanskrit syntax consists predominantly of relations between morphological categories. Some of the syntactic classes, though, are small and easily enumerable sets of words (such as prepositions, or adjectives that select the instrumental), and occasionally a single word will have a distinctive syntactic property. Consequently the syntactic list has to include: the categories (gender, case, number, tense-mood, voice, person); the combination patterns of categories (concord and government); and lists of words (such as prepositions) that govern particular cases. The patterns of government ('uses of the cases') can well be classified under the categories that constitute them. The concord patterns (subject-verb, adjective-noun/pronoun, participle-noun/pronoun, relative pronoun-antecedent) on the whole ought to be stated in a separate section. The lists of words should constitute a separate section, grouped according to syntactic properties ('verbs that govern two accusatives'), arranged alphabetically, and cross-indexed to the category and pattern sections. It is just as convenient, for reference, to arrange the categories and patterns topically as alphabetically, because the number of headings is quite small. Because these sections should be memorized, the topical arrangement is superior.

4.2. THE RULES. The rules will have to explain the composition of and interrelation between the lists, and give instructions for proceeding from the text to the lists—the analytic operations and their order. Explanation of the lists is quite straightforward. But the procedural instructions will be very complex, as the preceding discussion of analytic operations has indicated. Each instruction will have to be followed by a further pair between which the analyst must choose in accordance with the positive or negative result. 'Do A. If the result is X, then this problem is solved, and go on to the next one. If the result is Y, then the problem is not solved, and do B. If the result is ...' The order of the instructions is essential, but it need not be unique. Alternative sequences of rules may well be given, together with criteria for choosing between them if there is any basis for preference. This is in many ways the most interesting part of an analytic grammar. It makes the most demands on the ingenuity of the grammarian, and when well constructed it should be very satisfying esthetically. It is also very hard to plan without actually doing it, or to describe without actually presenting it. For these reasons I forego any attempt to say more about it here, except that it would be the second type of ordered-rule grammar for Sanskrit, the first being the chiefly synthetic grammar of the Paninean school created more than two millennia ago.

NOTES

1   Charles Rockwell Lanman, *A Sanskrit reader* (Boston, 1883).
2   Georg von der Gabelentz, 'Beitrag zur Geschichte der chinesischen Grammatik und zur Lehre von der grammatischen Behandlung der chinesischen Sprache', *Zeitschrift der Deutschen Morgenländischen Gesellschaft* 32.601–64 (1878).
3   Monier Monier-Williams, *A Sanskrit English dictionary* (London, 1872).
4   William Dwight Whitney, *A Sanskrit grammar*[2] (Cambridge, Mass., 1889); W. D. Whitney, *The roots, verb-forms, and primary derivatives of the Sanskrit language* (New Haven, Conn., 1945 [first printed Leipzig, 1885]).
5   Murray B. Emeneau, *Sanskrit sandhi and exercises* rev. ed. (Berkeley, 1958).

8

ON THE DATING OF NE *ee* AND *ea* SPELLINGS
FROM ME ę̄ AND ę̨́

Charles T. Scott

Historical phonology is principally concerned with two kinds of information: (1) the phonemic system of a language at any given point in its past history; and (2) the development of a particular phoneme or sequence of phonemes from one stage of a language's history to another, particularly when such developments result in changes in phonological systems. Since an earlier phonemic system is typically recoverable only through interpretation of written records, plus information from related languages and dialects and from subsequent developments in the language itself, the basic tool of the linguist for this task is a graphemic-phonemic analysis of historical documents. This is a reasonably safe procedure, especially when the writing system is primarily an alphabetic one, such as English has had through its entire history. For the linguist the underlying assumption is that earlier stages of an alphabetic writing system are apt to reflect a fairly close correspondence between phonemic entities and the orthographic devices used to represent those entities. The corollary to this assumption is that crystallization of spelling practices is still a long way from being complete.

Historical changes in the phonemic system of a language involve the addition and/or loss of phonemes through patterns known as mergers and splits. Crucial to the determination of changes in the phonemic system is an accurate chronology of those sound changes that bring about realignments in the phonological structure of the language between two different points in its history. But, since conclusions about phonemic changes can typically be reached only through the analysis and interpretation of written records, statements regarding the chronology of sound changes often depend in large measure on the chronological accuracy of certain spelling conventions and/or lapses. Statements of the latter sort commonly refer to dates when certain orthographic contrasts become fixed by printers and are thereafter regularly maintained, or to dates when otherwise conventional spellings are inadvertently violated by individuals, typically in such nonprinted documents as private letters. The date at which an orthographic contrast is fixed thus reflects a phonemic distinction at that point in the history of the language. Dates assigned to occasional spellings, such as *swit* for conventional *sweet*, may be interpreted as points in the history of a language when an earlier phonemic distinction has been lost or a new phonemic distinction has been made.

The purpose of this paper is twofold: (1) to state and discuss one methodological approach to the problem of dating spelling conventions; and (2) to date, as closely as possible, the actual fixing of NE *ee* and *ea* spellings derived from ME *ẹ̄* and *ẹ̄*. The earlier distinct vowel phonemes have, of course, since coalesced in NE /iy/, with the exception of such anomalous forms as *break*, *steak*, and *great*.

The spellings *ee* and *ea* are two of several graphs used to represent the complex nucleus /iy/ in NE. They are of interest to the historian of English phonology since they are the orthographic derivatives of ME *ẹ̄* and *ẹ̄* and, as such, attest an earlier stage in the pronunciation of the English vowels when words deriving from ME *ẹ̄* were in phonemic contrast with words deriving from ME *ẹ̄*. The graphic contrast which has been preserved in present-day English orthography has, of course, no relevance to the NE pronunciation. Neither does the graphic contrast serve any useful purpose in terms of morpheme identity (an argument which may have some legitimate bearing on our preservation of *night* and *knight* for the homophonous forms /nayt/ and /nayt/), since those morphemes which are orthographically distinguished by *ee* and *ea*, although homophonous, generally do not show the same syntactic distribution, and hence cause no confusion.

While deviant spellings are often of value to the historian of phonology, regularly maintained orthographic contrasts in the earlier recorded history of a language can be particularly useful (1) as evidence of phonemic contrast, and (2) with less certainty, as possible evidence for phonetic interpretation. This presupposes, however, that the linguist has sufficiently reliable external evidence to assume that the orthography had not reached a stage of complete petrification, that development toward the crystallization of spelling was still in process but had not been completed, that, in short, the orthography still reflects the attempt to employ different graphs for different sounds, not merely to differentiate homophonous morphemes. With enough external evidence to support such a situation, the linguist then has justification for a procedural assumption that permits him to cite spelling changes as evidence for pronunciation changes, or at least as evidence for new oppositions in the phonemic system. For these reasons the NE spellings *ee* and *ea* (in words like *seek*, *feet*, *deep*; *deal*, *teach*, *lead*; etc.) are of interest to the historian of English phonology. While they no longer represent a phonemic contrast in English, the different spellings bear witness to a stage in the history of English phonology when they did represent a contrast.

But the mere evidence of an earlier phonemic distinction is of minor interest. The question of dating the phonemic distinction is much more crucial, since no reconstruction of sound changes is particularly illuminating unless the chronology of the sound changes can also be determined. We should like to know exactly when it was that words deriving from ME *ę̄* and *ę̄* were first clearly and consistently distinguished by the spellings *ee* and *ea*, respectively. The procedural assumption is that, if a date can be fixed for this sharp separation of spellings, that same date can be assigned to a stage in the history of English phonology when the two graphs represented a contrast in the phonemic system of the language: *ee* probably representing /ih/, since we know that this raising phenomenon took place quite early, and *ea* probably representing /eh/.[1] We would then have a sure point of departure from which we could move forward chronologically in our efforts to date more precisely the falling in of /eh/ with /ih/, both ultimately becoming NE /iy/. In dating the eventual coalescence, however, the orthography would no longer be useful, since the orthographic distinction has been petrified in our NE spelling and seems destined to remain so for a long time to come.

The immediate problem, however, is simply one of dating an orthographic distinction that has been preserved in NE. As such, it is a problem directly relevant to early spelling and printing practices rather than to the reconstruction of earlier stages of pronunciation. For this reason an examination of the works of such historians as Wyld, Zachrisson, Dobson, Jespersen, and Kökeritz would prove largely unproductive, since their concern has been to reconstruct the history of English sound changes, not spelling practices.[2] To be sure, Wyld and Zachrisson make considerable use of occasional spellings as supporting evidence for certain of the sound changes which they reconstruct, and Jespersen clearly indicates that he is willing to assign a phonetic interpretation to original *ea* spellings, but this use of spellings as evidence for sound changes does not in any way represent a precise chronological reconstruction of English spelling practices. Wyld, for example, already proves his point when he cites occasional spellings like *agryd* and *symed* to show that at a particular date ME *ę̄* has been raised to /ih/. In other words, there is no need for him to pursue the matter of the changing and the fixing of the spelling to *ee* in NE. It would appear, then, that the major historians of English phonology cannot help in this problem of dating precisely the separation of *ee* and *ea* spellings.

Available orthoepical evidence also fails to throw any light on *ee* and *ea* spellings. It is again negative: (1) because the earliest orthoepical evidence available appeared in the late sixteenth century when *ee* and *ea* spellings were already in vogue, and were beginning to be used with some consistency; and (2) because the orthoepists, for the most part, were themselves spelling reformers. Like their twentieth-century counterparts, they labored just as futilely to arrest the increasing gap between English orthography and English pronunciation. Their evidence, of course, is often of considerable value in terms of reconstructing pronunciation features. However, attempts on their part to level *ee* and *ea* spellings under a single graph, say *ee*, show only that words derived from ME $\bar{e}$ had already begun to a great extent to be pronounced like words derived from ME $\bar{e}$.

The separation of *ee* and *ea* spellings was beginning to be maintained with some consistency during the latter part of the sixteenth century. Jespersen (1909, 1.4) suggests that the sixteenth- and seventeenth-century spellings in printed books were comparatively fixed, by which he means that, while some uniformity in spelling was beginning to be achieved by the printing houses, considerable spelling fluctuation could still be found in private documents and letters of the time. It is from spellings culled from nonprinted sources that Wyld and Zachrisson draw much of their orthographic evidence for explaining sound changes. This implies that the printers had already made headway in fixing the orthography, as far as they were concerned, and that the rapid changes in pronunciation taking place during the early NE period were already creating an obvious lag in orthographic practices. Jespersen notes that in ME no spelling distinction was made between $\bar{e}$ and $\bar{e}$. The graphs used to represent both sounds were *e* or *ee*. In the sixteenth century, however, an orthographic distinction evolved: $\bar{e}$ was written as *ee*, *e*, or *ei*; $\bar{e}$ was written as *ea* or *e——e* (Jespersen, 1909, 1.76). Dobson (1957, 2.645) notes that *ea* spellings began to appear in the fifteenth century, and became gradually more common in the early part of the sixteenth century. By the end of that century, the orthographic distinction was being made with consistency by the printers.

A sample check of known derivatives of ME $\bar{e}$ and $\bar{e}$ should verify this conclusion and determine if a more precise date might be established for the separation of *ee* and *ea* spellings. The words *beetle, deem, deep, flee, free, geese, green,* and *seek* are representative examples of NE words derived from ME $\bar{e}$. The words *cheap, clean, deal, lead, leap, sea,* and *speak* are examples of NE words derived from ME $\bar{e}$. The particular selection of the words themselves (aside from being known derivatives) is of no importance, since words deriving from the same source would behave, or be treated in the same way, in the process of stabilizing their orthography. The obvious source to check these words is the *Oxford English dictionary*, in spite of the fact that its citations are grouped chronologically on the basis of semantic differentiation. In this paper, however, only the spellings of the citations are of interest.

If a date is noted, beyond which all subsequent citations consistently show either *ee* or *ea* spellings, then that date can be regarded as a pretty clear indication as to when the spellings were actually and finally adopted by the printing houses. The date itself can only be regarded as approximate, since the actual separation of spellings might have been fixed shortly before, or shortly after, the date assigned. The important thing is that the date selected is not necessarily the one corresponding to the first citation showing an *ee* or *ea* spelling. For instance, some *ee* and *ea* spellings can be noted for fourteenth-century citations. These may be dismissed as coincidental fluctuations, since later citations revert to other spellings.

The results obtained from examination of this sample confirm the general observations of Jespersen and Dobson. The *ee* and *ea* spellings can be dated as follows:

beetle	(1589)	*cheap*	(1567)
deem	(1581)	*clean*	(1568)
deep	(1560)	*deal*	(1534)
flee	(1600)	*lead*	(1569)
free	(1580)	*leap*	(1580)
geese	(1577)	*sea*	(1555)
green	(1578)	*speak*	(1535)
seek	(1590)		

Although the greatest clustering of these dates is in the last quarter of the sixteenth century, the dates themselves range over a period of 66 years, a span which probably verifies only two things: (1) that the orthographic distinction between *ee* and *ea* was finally made toward the end of the sixteenth century; and (2) that the clear separation of spellings was an achievement reached only gradually by the printing houses. Such conclusions lead to a dating which is probably as precise as we can realistically hope for.

Krapp suggests that the origins of a rigidly uniform system of spelling are to be found in the rise of the great printing houses in England in the eighteenth century.[3] This would seem to corroborate the opinions of most historians of the English language that NE spelling was fixed almost completely by Dr. Johnson's dictionary of 1755. But fluctuation in the spelling of *ee* and *ea* words had been checked well before the middle of the eighteenth century. McKnight notes that the chief difference (and one of the major points of progress toward modernization of spelling in the seventeenth century) between the first and second folio editions of Shakespeare's works is the regularly established distinction made between *i* and *j*, and *u* and *v*.[4] If the settling of these spelling conventions is actually one of the last major developments in the regularization of English spelling, then there is justification for assuming that the separation of *ee* and *ea* spellings had already been fixed.

No further light on the separation of *ee* and *ea* spellings is provided by evidence from the dictionaries, since the first dictionary which intentionally aimed to include *all* English words was Nathan Bailey's,[5] which did not appear until 1721, better than a century after the *ee* and *ea* spellings were pretty firmly established by the practice of the printing houses. The seventeenth-century dictionaries were all 'hard word' dictionaries, and therefore extremely restrictive in their inclusion of entries.[6]

If it were particularly necessary to date the adoption of *ee* and *ea* spellings even more exactly, the procedure presumably would be to examine a sufficiently large sampling of major books (first editions) published by the important printing houses during the latter half of the sixteenth century.[7] The tediousness of such a task, though, and the cost involved in letting a computer do the text-searching, might not actually prove anything more conclusive or more illuminating, for the purposes of historical phonology, than the information obtained from the small sample of known derivatives of ME ę̄ and ẹ̄ presented above.

The fact clearly emerges that in the latter part of the sixteenth century words deriving from ME ę̄ and ẹ̄ were phonemically distinct, and that the eventual coalescence of /ih/ and /eh/ was accomplished later than this period, perhaps as late as the eighteenth century as Wyld suggests (1927. 171). Since the *ee/ea* orthographic contrast has been maintained to the present day, however, any attempt to date the final completion of this coalescence must be made from evidence other than the kind which has been considered in this paper. In part, such evidence can still be drawn from the orthography, but, from the beginning of the seventeenth century, this evidence will be restricted to the examination of rhymes and occasional spellings, since the value of using the regularly maintained orthographic contrast has now been exhausted.

NOTES

1 In writing /ih/ and /eh/, I follow Robert P. Stockwell's interpretation of earlier phonemic oppositions in English in Trager-Smith terms: two types of vocalic contrasts—simple vowels and complex nuclei. Short vowels are simple vowels, long vowels are sequences of simple vowels and semivowels, the /h/ here designating a centralizing glide. See Stockwell's 'The Middle English "long close" and "long open" mid vowels', *Texas studies in literature and language* 2.529–38 (Austin, 1960–1). Historians of English phonology generally agree that ME ẹ̄ was raised to a high-front articulatory position at least as early as 1550.

2 H. C. Wyld, *A short history of English*, 3rd rev. ed. (New York, 1927); R. E. Zachrisson, *Pronunciation of English vowels, 1400–1700* (Göteborg, 1913); E. J. Dobson, *English pronunciation, 1500–1700*, 2 vols. (Oxford, Eng., 1957); Otto Jespersen, *A modern English grammar on historical principles*, vol. 1

(Heidelberg, 1909); and Helge Kökeritz, *Shakespeare's pronunciation* (New Haven, 1953).

3 George Philip Krapp, *Modern English, its growth and present use* 172 (New York, 1909).
4 George H. McKnight, *Modern English in the making* 241 (New York, 1928).
5 Nathan Bailey, *An universal etymological English dictionary* (London, 1721).
6 Robert Cawdrey, *A table alphabeticall* (London, 1604); John Bullokar, *An English expositor* (London, 1616); Henry Cockeram, *The English dictionarie* (London, 1623); Thomas Blount, *Glossographia* (London, 1656); Edward Phillips, *The new world of English words* (London, 1658); and Elisha Coles, *An English dictionary* (London, 1676).
7 The source for this sampling would undoubtedly be R. B. McKerrow, gen. ed., *A dictionary of printers and booksellers in England, Scotland, and Ireland, and of foreign printers of English books, 1577–1640*, Bibliographical Society monographs no. 13 (London, 1910)

9

A CONTRASTIVE DESCRIPTION
OF PENNSYLVANIA GERMAN AND STANDARD GERMAN
STOPS AND FRICATIVES

Lester W. J. Seifert

In the past decade or so, a new aspect of descriptive linguistics has been rapidly developing, namely contrastive grammar. To be sure, contrastive studies of a sort are at least as old as comparative grammar, but these earlier studies were largely hit-or-miss affairs, dealing only with isolated bits taken from the totality of the structure of a given language. A notable and still valuable exception is found in J. Ferdinand Sommer's *Vergleichende Syntax der Schulsprachen (Deutsch, Englisch, Französisch, Griechisch, Lateinisch) mit besonderer Berücksichtigung des Deutschen.*[1] In this work, as in modern contrastive descriptions, he attempts to deal systematically with a large, related complex of linguistic phenomena.

The word 'Schulsprachen' in Sommer's title is of more than passing interest; it was, so to speak, prophetic of the way in which contrastive grammar was to develop a quarter of a century or so later. Modern contrastive grammar is, for the most part, concerned with problems connected with second-language teaching and learning, i.e. it has received its chief impetus from applied linguistics. In one sense this is unfortunate, although we are naturally happy with any development that makes foreign-language instruction more effective. This emphasis on practical matters has caused us to neglect the possibilities that contrastive descriptions hold for bringing linguistic structures into clear focus. The purpose of this paper is to show such possibilities by contrasting the stop and fricative consonant systems of Pennsylvania German and Standard German.[2]

Both StG and PaG have a set of six stop phonemes that we may symbolize with the letters /p t k/ and /b d g/. In both StG and PaG the /p/ and /b/ are bilabial, the /t/ and /d/ are dentals, the /k/ and /g/ have palatal and velar allophones depending on the type of vowel (or consonant) with which they are in contact: palatal in such a word as StG /'kü:e/, PaG /ki:/ 'cows'; velar in StG /ku:/, PaG /ku:/ 'cow'. But this is the end of the similarities of these consonants, as a set, in StG and PaG. The primary opposition between the subset /p t k/ and the subset /b d g/ in

StG is voicelessness and voice, respectively, with the secondary opposition
of aspiration and nonaspiration, respectively. In PaG the primary opposition between the two subsets is fortis versus lenis; the secondary opposition
of aspiration versus nonaspiration remains.

These two subsets have a very different distribution in StG and PaG.
The voiceless /p t k/ of StG can occur initially, medially, and finally:
/'pasen/ 'fit, be suitable', /'tapfer/ 'brave', /ga:p/ 'gave'; /tu:n/ 'do',
/'biter/ 'bitter', /ta:t/ 'did'; /kalt/ 'cold', /'baken/ 'bake', /ta:k/ 'day'.
The voiced /b d g/ of StG, on the other hand, can occur only initially and
medially: /balt/ 'soon', /'ge:ben/ 'give'; /da:/ 'there', /'to:des/ 'of death';
/golt/ 'gold', /'ta:ge/ 'days'. In PaG, fortis /p t k/ can occur only in initial
position: /pan/ 'pan', /kald/ 'cold'. PaG /t/ needs a special statement. Of
words that are commonly used, it occurs in only three that are natively
German: /te:/[3] 'tea', /tud/[4] 'paper bag' (StG 'Tüte'), /'tu:de/ 'blow a
horn'. There are, however, numerous words borrowed from English in
which the initial /t/ is retained, e.g. /'ti:dše/ 'teach', /'tombler/ 'water
glass'.

The PaG lenis subset of /b d g/ has free occurrence initially, medially,
and finally: /bi:r/ 'beer', /'bobel/ 'baby', /da:b/[5] 'deaf'; /da:/ 'there',
/'dade/ 'there', /do:d/ 'dead'; /gans/ 'goose', /'gagere/ 'cackle', /da:g/
'day'.

At this point it is already evident that the functions of the two subsets
of stop consonants are reversed in StG and PaG. StG voiceless /p t k/
have the same freedom of occurrence as PaG lenis /b d g/; StG voiced
/b d g/ and PaG fortis /p t k/ are restricted in occurrence, but the restrictions are more stringent in PaG than in StG. But there is another part of
the picture—the way in which these stop consonants can enter into con-
tactual sequences with other consonants.

StG voiceless /p t k/ combine with certain other consonants initially:
/p/ with /f s l r/, as in /'pfaefe/ 'pipe', /psalm/ 'psalm', /plats/ 'place,
square', /praes/ 'price, prize'; /t/ with /s r/, as in /tsaet/ 'time', /troi/ 'faith-
ful'; /k/ with /s l n r/, as in /'ksanten/ 'Xanten', /kla:r/ 'clear', /knext/
'servant', /kri:k/ 'war'. The StG /p t k/ are involved in some three-
consonantal initial sequences: /'pflantse/ 'plant', /pfropf/ 'cork', /'šprexen/
'speak', /'štroien/ 'strew, scatter', /'skla:ve/ 'slave', /ˌskri:'bent/ 'hack
writer'.

Final consonant sequences with /p t k/ are even more numerous. The
following examples are not intended to be exhaustive: /gipt/ 'gives',
/za:kt/ 'says', /zaft/ 'juice', /ʔist/ 'is', /lant/ 'land, country', /golt/
'gold', /bart/ 'beard', /zats/ 'sentence', /doitš/ 'German'; /halp/ 'half',
/herp/ 'bitter, astringent', /ʔa:pt/ 'abbot', /tsopf/ 'braid of hair', /krips/
'back of the neck' (North German colloquial), /kampf/ 'battle', /kompt/
'comes', /knirps/ 'little rascal', /herpst/ 'autumn'; /daŋk/ 'thanks'

(noun), /talk/ 'tallow', /berk/ 'mountain, hill'; /daŋkt/ 'thanks' (verb), /ʔakt/ 'act of a play', /zeks/ 'six', /zaːkst/ 'you (sing.) say', /zorkst/ 'you (sing.) worry, take care of', /velkt/ 'withers', /velkst/ 'you (sing.) wither (away)'.

StG voiced /b d g/ do not have the same freedom of entering into consonant sequences. All three occur initially in sequences with /r/, only /b/ and /g/ with /l/: /braon/ 'brown', /drae/ 'three', /grao/ 'gray'; /blao/ 'blue', /glat/ 'smooth, slippery'. There are no final sequences with /b d g/ in StG.

The occurrence of the PaG stop phonemes in consonant sequences is quite different from that noted above for StG. PaG fortis /p t k/ can occur only initially and only directly before vocalic phonemes: /pan/ 'pan', /tud/ 'paper bag', /kald/ 'cold'. However, PaG lenis /b d g/ enter into a number of consonantal sequences: (1) initially, as in /bloː/ 'blue', /gleː/ 'small', /šbids/ 'point', /šdad/ 'city, town', /šblid/ 'split, crack' (noun), /šglaːf/ 'slave', /brao/ 'brown', /drae/ 'three', /groː/ 'gray', /gnob/ 'button', /šbrao/ 'chaff', /šdroː/ 'straw'; (2) finally, as in /kalb/ 'calf', /šdrumb/ 'stocking', /šbiːld/ 'plays', /blaebd/ 'stays', /draːgd/ 'carries', /fexd/ 'fight, brawl' (noun), /ˈgšwišderd/ 'siblings', /deŋd/ 'thinks', /wašd/ 'sausage', /segšd/ 'sixth', /šbiːlšd/ 'you (sing.) play', /blaebšd/ 'you (sing.) stay', /draːgšd/ 'you (sing.) carry', /deŋšd/ 'you (sing.) think'.

Although both StG and PaG have six stop phonemes, the two subsets of three each differ radically in their primary opposition, namely, voicelessness versus voice in StG, fortis versus lenis in PaG. Secondly, in StG voiceless /p t k/ bear a heavier functional burden, occur in more words, and in more positions within a word than voiced /b d g/. In PaG the lenis /b d g/ carry a heavy functional load, while the burden of the fortis /p t k/ is very light. The status of PaG /t/, in particular, is precarious; perhaps it continues to exist only because of the support coming from English loanwords.

One other difference exists between these sets of six stop phonemes. In StG there is a very frequent morphophonemic alternation between /p/ and /b/, between /t/ and /d/, and between /k/ and /g/: /gaːp/ 'gave' ~ /ˈgeːben/ 'give', /raːt/ 'wheel' ~ /ˈreːder/ 'wheels', /taːk/ 'day' ~ /ˈtaːge/ 'days'. This particular type of morphophonemic alternation cannot occur in PaG, because fortis /p t k/ are restricted to initial positions in a word, while lenis /b d g/ have freedom of occurrence in initial, medial, and final positions. PaG /g/ enters into a different type of morphophonemic alternation, and is discussed below.

The next set of consonants consists of the fricatives. In StG there is a set of six that is like the set of six stops in that these fricatives fall into two

subsets with the primary opposition of voicelessness and voice—voiceless
/f s š/ and voiced /v z ž/.[6] In regard to distribution, however, the fricative
subsets do not operate in the same way as the stop subsets. Voiceless /f/
and /š/, like voiceless /p t k/, to be sure, can occur initially, medially, and
finally: /fiš/ 'fish', /'hofen/ 'hope', /hoːf/ 'yard, court'; /'šuːle/ 'school',
/'vašen/ 'wash', /tiš/ 'table'. Initial, voiceless /s/, on the other hand, can
occur only in southern varieties of StG: /soː/ 'so, thus', /siː/ 'she, they',
but elsewhere /zoː/ and /ziː/. Medially, as in /'visen/ 'know', and finally,
as in /vaes/ 'knows, white', voiceless /s/ occurs in all varieties of StG.
There is another important distributional difference between /f/ and /s/.
The latter cannot enter into initial consonant sequences except in relatively
small areas of northwestern Germany, where it is possible to say /'slaŋe/
'snake', /smaːl/ 'narrow', /sneː/ 'snow', /spits/ 'sharp, pointed', /staen/
'stone', /'svimen/ 'swim', instead of using the initial /š/ that is common
elsewhere.[7] In all varieties of StG, initial /f/ enters freely into /l/ and /r/
sequences: /'fliːgen/ 'fly', /frae/ 'free'. For examples of /pf/ and the particularly numerous final sequences involving /s/, see the discussion of stops
above. Also /f/ enters into a fair number of final sequences, e.g. /fünf/[8]
'five', /half/ 'helped', /dorf/ 'village', /kampf/ 'battle', /ʔoft/ 'often',
/dürft/ 'you (pl.) may, ought', /darfst/ 'you (sing.) may, ought'.

   StG voiced /v z ž/ can occur only initially and medially: /'vaser/
'water', /'löːve/ 'lion'; /zoː/ 'so, thus', /'vaeze/ 'wise'; /ˌžurˈnaːl/ 'journal',
/ˌgaˈraːže/ 'garage'. In this aspect of distribution, /v z ž/ are like the
voiced stops /b d g/, but in another aspect they are markedly different.
Voiced /b g/ enter into initial sequences with /l/, and /b d g/ with /r/,
as in examples above. Voiced /v/, however, enters into initial sequences
only with /r/, and then only in two words: /vrak/ 'wreckage of a ship',
/'vriŋen/ 'wring out clothes'.[9] As far as I know, there is no variety of StG
in which voiced /z ž/ enter into initial sequences with either /l/ or /r/,
or, for that matter, with any other consonant.

   The pattern of morphophonemic alternation is also different for StG
stops and fricatives. With the stops (see above) all three possible alternating
pairs occur: /gaːp/ ∼ /'geːben/, /raːt/ ∼ /'reːder/, /taːk/ ∼ /'taːge/.
With the fricatives, voiceless /s/ alternates with voiced /z/: /maos/
'mouse' ∼ /'moize/ 'mice', /raest/ 'travels' ∼ /'raezen/ 'travel'. But
again, as far as I know, there are no such alternating pairs involving
voiceless /f š/ and voiced /v ž/. An alternation of the type /volf/ 'wolf' ∼
/'völve/ 'wolves' does not occur; in other words, the voiceless /f/ is retained
in the plural form /'völfe/.

   The PaG fricatives provide a completely different situation. Where
StG has a set of six fricative phonemes, /f s š/ and /v z ž/, PaG has a set
of only four, /f s š/ and /w/. There are no PaG lenis equivalents of StG

voiced /z ž/; thus the well-balanced system of equivalents that obtains in
the case of the stop phonemes does not carry over to the fricative phonemes.
PaG does have a fortis /s/ as the equivalent of StG voiceless /s/, but this
fortis /s/ occurs initially, medially, and finally; hence it has greater freedom
of occurrence than StG voiceless /s/, which is restricted to medial and final
positions. PaG examples are: /sel/ 'that' (dem.), /'waser/ 'water', /he:s/
'hot'. PaG /s/ does not enter into initial consonant sequences except after
/d/, as in /dsaed/ 'time', or after /g/, as in /gsa:d/ 'said' (past ptc. = StG
'gesagt'). In final position, it frequently follows lenis /d g/: /hads/[10]
'heart', /'barigs/ 'credit' (/uf 'barigs 'ka:fe/ 'to buy on credit'). It rarely
follows lenis /b/: /gibs/ 'gypsum, plaster of Paris', /gnærbs/ 'little fellow,
little rascal'.[11]

PaG /š/, like StG /š/, occurs initially, medially, and finally: /šu:l/
'school', /'waše/ 'wash', /diš/ 'table'. There are numerous initial consonant
sequences in which /š/ precedes, follows, or comes between other consonants: /šbads/ 'sparrow', /šdad/ 'town, city', /šgla:f/ 'slave', /šbrao/
'chaff', /šdro:/ 'straw', /šmals/[12] 'lard', /šne:/ 'snow', /'šlo:fe/ 'sleep',
/šraewe/ 'write', /'bšaese/[13] 'cheat', /'bšli:se/ 'conclude', /'bšraewe/
'describe', /gšafd/ 'worked, operated' (past ptc.), /'gšdane/ 'stood',
/'gšmise/ 'thrown', /gšne:t/ 'snowed', /'gšlo:fe/ 'slept', /'gšriwe/ 'written',
/gšwišderd/ 'siblings'. In final consonant sequences, /š/ occurs in clusters
of two or three phonemes: /wešb/ 'wasp', /wašd/[14] 'sausage', /hibš/
'pretty', /daedš/ 'German', /segšd/ 'sixth', /šbi:lšd/ 'you (sing.) play',
/blaebšd/ 'you (sing.) stay', /dra:gšd/ 'you (sing.) carry', /deŋšd/ 'you
(sing.) think'.

PaG /f/, as in StG, also occurs initially, medially, and finally: /fu:s/
'foot', /'hofe/ 'hope', /paef/ 'pipe'. There are initial consonant sequences
with /l/ and /r/: /'fli:je/ 'fly', /fra:/ 'woman, wife'. There is one final
consonant sequence with lenis /d/, as in /ofd/ 'often', /hofd/ 'hopes'.
There is no PaG consonant sequence equivalent to the /pf/ that is so
common in StG.

A PaG lenis equivalent of StG voiced /v/ does not exist. Instead of the
StG voiced labio-dental fricative /v/, PaG has a lenis bilabial fricative
/w/. Like StG voiced labio-dental /v/, PaG lenis bilabial /w/ can occur
only initially and medially: /'waser/ 'water', /'gewe/ 'give'. It enters into
initial consonant sequences following /g/ and /š/: /gwinšd/[15] 'wished'
(past ptc.), /'šwime/ 'swim'.

There is no possibility of morphophonemic alternation in PaG as far as
the stop consonants are concerned (see above), since PaG fortis /p t k/
are restricted to initial positions in a word. Also, there can be no morphophonemic alternations involving the PaG fortis fricatives /s/ and /š/,
although they occur initially, medially, and finally, because there are no

lenis equivalents of these phonemes. The PaG lenis bilabial fricative /w/ does enter into three different morphophonemic alternations:

1. with ø: /buː/ 'boy' ∼ /'buːwe/[16] 'boys';
2. with /b/: /šiːbd/ 'shoves, pushes' ∼ /'šiːwe/ 'shove, push', /leːb/ 'lion' ∼ /'leːwe/ 'lions', /doːbd/ 'rages' ∼ /'doːwe/ 'rage', /šaːb/ 'moth' ∼ /'šaːwe/ 'moths', /kalb/ 'calf' ∼ /'kelwer/ 'calves', /šdarbd/ 'dies' ∼ /'šdarwe/[17] 'die', /raebd/ 'rubs' ∼ /'raewe/ 'rub', /šraobd/ 'screws' ∼ /'šraowe/ 'screw';
3. with /g/, but only for a minority of speakers and then in the eastern and northern parts of the PaG area: /bluːgd/ 'plows' ∼ /'bluːwe/ 'plow', /froːgd/ 'asks' ∼ /'froːwe/ 'ask', /saːgd/[18] 'says' ∼ /saːwe/[19] 'say'. The alternation /g/ ∼ /w/ can occur only after the tense back vowels, while the alternation /b/ ∼ /w/ has no comparable restrictions.

This triple morphophonemic alternation of the PaG lenis bilabial fricative /w/ with ø, with the lenis bilabial stop /b/, and with the lenis velar stop /g/ is a feature that I have found in no other variety of German. Perhaps it is the result of the processes of dialect-leveling that gave rise to PaG, or perhaps it is an independent development that occurred only after the emergence of the PaG dialect.[20]

In this paper I have attempted to bring the following points into clear focus: (1) there is some agreement between PaG and StG as far as their subsystems of stops and fricatives are concerned; (2) the areas of disagreement, however, between PaG and StG stops and fricatives are much more extensive than those of agreement; (3) points 1 and 2 are true both in the phonetic realizations of the phonemes involved and in the varying distributional patterns of the occurrence of these phonemes; (4) differences in the morphophonemic alternations that occur in PaG and StG stops and fricatives are particularly striking.

NOTES

1   Third ed. (Leipzig, 1931).
2   Pennsylvania German is spoken in the southeastern part of Pennsylvania in a large, roughly elliptical area stretching from Northampton and Bucks counties in the east to Centre and Mifflin counties in the west, from Lancaster and York counties in the south to Northumberland and Union counties in the north. There may be close to 200,000 speakers of the dialect in this main area, with another 100,000 in smaller settlements scattered in the rest of Pennsylvania, in Maryland, Virginia, Ohio, Indiana, Illinois, and Iowa. In recent years, two settlements have been established in Wisconsin.

PaG is basically a Franconian dialect of the Palatine with considerable Alemannic influences and with numerous borrowings from English. Although PaG is by no means completely homogeneous over the entire area in which it is spoken, the differences are not great enough to hinder easy communication; in this paper the usage of Lehigh County is generally followed. Many of the examples are taken from the phonetic field recordings made in 1940 and 1941 by Carroll E. Reed (the University of Washington) and myself, with some supplemental recordings made in more recent years. There are copies of these recordings at the University of Michigan (in the collections of the 'Linguistic atlas of the United States and Canada'), the University of Washington, and the University of Wisconsin.

My phonemic analysis differs somewhat from that given by Carroll E. Reed, *The Pennsylvania German dialect spoken in the counties of Lehigh and Berks: Phonology and morphology* (Seattle, 1949), but in the framework of this paper these differences need not be argued. The citations in Standard German are based on a northern variety unless otherwise specified; the phonemic transcription differs considerably from that found in such a widely used book as William G. Moulton, *The sounds of English and German* (Chicago, 1962). For the purpose of this paper it is unnecessary to decide whether StG is a fiction. Neither does it seem necessary to describe the steps taken to arrive at the phonemicization here used for PaG and StG.

3   It is, of course, 'native' only in an extended meaning of the word, in the sense that *Tee* has been used for several centuries in all varieties of German.

4   In the PaG area as a whole, the form /dud/ is more common than /tud/. For a fair number of speakers the vocalic nucleus is /u:/. Cf. Map 35 in Reed and Seifert, *A linguistic atlas of Pennsylvania German* (Marburg, 1954) for the distribution of /d-/ and /t-/.

5   Phonetically, /a:/ is realized as a tense (long), low-back, rounded vowel.

6   The fact that /ž/ is a phoneme borrowed from French and used only in loanwords is of no concern here.

7   The currency of these words with an initial /s/ varies considerably. Perhaps the area south and east of Hamburg has the longest list of such words.

8   For many North Germans, however, this numeral is /fümpf/.

9   Even these words may be considered as borrowings from those North German dialects that have maintained /vr-/.

10   For many speakers, the structure of this word (and of others like it) is /hards/, where /r/ is realized as a uvular scrape, or the /a/ is co-articulated with constriction of the musculature in the back of the mouth so that there is simultaneous audible friction. These observations also hold true for the realization and occurrence of /r/ in the final, unaccented syllable /er/, as in /'waser/ 'water'. For somewhat different statements of these facts, cf. Reed (1949) 28, and Albert F. Buffington and Preston A. Barba, *A Pennsylvania German grammar* 6 and 8 (Allentown, 1954).

11   Both of these words are really relics, but they are listed as 'gips' (65) and 'knærps' (94) in Marcus B. Lambert, *A dictionary of the non-English words of the Pennsylvania-German dialect*, Proceedings and addresses, The Pennsylvania-German Society vol. 30 (Lancaster, 1924). In compounds, there are a few of

the type /ˌkobs ˈfederšd/ 'headfirst'; cf. Lambert (95) under 'kopps-'. Because of syllabification problems, I have in this paper avoided examples with medial consonant sequences.

12   This word has an interesting regional distribution in contrast with /fed/; cf. Reed and Seifert, Map 70.

13   For many speakers, however, this word is /be ˈšaese/, also /be ˈšliːse/ and /be ˈšraewe/.

14   But for some speakers it is /waršd/; cf. note 10.

15   The form is /ge ˈwinšd/ for the majority of speakers except in the southwestern part of the PaG dialect area; cf. Reed and Seifert, Map 61.

16   This type of alternation is rare, perhaps even limited to this one word.

17   A rather small minority of speakers has the accented vowel /æ/ in this word.

18   A relic form of this word is /sexd/.

19   For most speakers of PaG, this morphophonemic alternation involves /g/ ∼ /j/, thus: /bluːgd/ ∼ /ˈbluːje/, /froːgd/ ∼ /froːje/, /saːgd/ ∼ /ˈsaːje/; cf. Reed (1949) 29. For another small minority, there is no alternation in these and similar words: /bluːgd/, /ˈbluːge/, etc.

20   The two phonemes /h/ and /x/, occurring in both PaG and StG, need no special treatment, since they agree in both varieties as to phonetic realization and patterns of occurrence. The examples in this paper indicate that I consider the one phoneme /x/ to have two allophones, the one palatal, the other velar. I have no hesitation about following the suggestion that was first (I believe) openly made by Werner F. Leopold in his short but important article 'German ch', *Language* 24.179–180 (1948). Not only do speakers of German (Pa or St) learn that there is a diminutive suffix /-xen/, but also that this suffix always occurs with the palatal allophone of the fricative regardless of the phonetic quality of the preceding phoneme.

10

METHODOLOGY
IN IMMEDIATE CONSTITUENT ANALYSIS

John C. Street

When a linguist attempts his first, preliminary analysis of a hitherto undescribed language, his most important procedures are those of segmentation, differentiation, and grouping;[1] these procedures are applied on several different structural strata. On all strata it is clear that organization is hierarchical rather than simply linear; that is, within any one stratum one may focus on chunks of various sizes, such that the chunks on one given size-level (except the smallest) are combinations of chunks on the next smaller size-level.[2] Thus, on the phonological stratum, for example, a chunk /p/ may be viewed as a single element of one sort (a phoneme), as a combination of smaller elements (distinctive features), or as part of a larger element (a syllable or—still larger—a macrosegment) such as /pæt/. Similarly, on the morphological stratum a chunk *the cat* may be viewed as a noun phrase, as a combination of determiner plus noun, or as a part (object of a preposition) of an utterance such as *Don't step on the cat*. The existence of such different-sized chunks requires, or at least makes convenient, the recognition of different tactic or combinatory levels[3] within any given stratum.

Traditional grammar gives explicit recognition to hierarchical organization only in the area of syntax; various systems for the visual representation of such organization—systems for parsing or diagramming—began to be developed at least as early as 1847.[4] In such systems, as generally, traditional grammar relied more on the native speaker's intuitions than on formally stated criteria or definitions.

American structuralists, on the other hand, faced with numerous languages of which they were not native speakers, were forced to seek some sort of nonintuitive (or at least less than fully intuitive) principles by which they could discover and describe at least the general outlines of syntactic structures. The result, during the second quarter of the present century, was the theory of IMMEDIATE CONSTITUENTS (=ICs) 'originally set forth by Bloomfield, provided with exegesis by Pike, and systematized by Wells'.[5] Compared with Wells's now-classic article,[6] Bloomfield's use of ICs[7] was most unsystematic, and even Pike's 1943 article[8]—a valuable clarification at that time—strikes us today as little more than an overt statement of some of our stronger intuitions about hierarchical structure in morphology and syntax. Wells managed to state at least some of the distributional factors underlying such intuitions, and linguists spent some time digesting his insights and experimentally applying his theory of IC analysis to various languages. Almost immediately, too, IC analysis began to be applied to hierarchical structures on the phonological stratum.[9]

By the middle 1950's enough had become known about individual problems of language structure and linguistic theory so that linguists began to turn their attention to the broader, metatheoretic problems of models for linguistic analysis. Their metatheorizing inevitably has had effects on individual aspects of earlier theory, such as IC analysis.

The present article briefly reexamines 'classical' IC theory, discusses some modifications of the theory which have been suggested in the past decade or so, and concludes with some remarks about the use of IC analysis as a tool in preliminary language description.

1. CONSTITUTES AND IMMEDIATE CONSTITUENTS. Let us assume we have collected a corpus of utterances in a particular language, and that we are able to identify most morphemes. Clearly the relationships between all possible pairs of morphemes in a given utterance are not the same; even our limited knowledge of the language tells us, for example, that morphemes *d* and *e* form some kind of unit, that morpheme *a* seems somehow to 'go together' with the sequence *bc*, and that the whole utterance appears to have a major break after morpheme *g*. We can then approach segmentation in either of two ways: we may go from morpheme to utterance, by successively grouping together morphemes or morpheme sequences whose relations seem particularly close, or we may go from utterance to morpheme, cutting successively smaller sequences into parts at what seem like major points of cleavage. In either case we arrive at a segmentation of the utterance into its layered constituents; whether we group two elements into one larger whole or cut a sequence into smaller pieces we are dealing with a CONSTITUTE (the larger whole) and its ICs.[10] The IC partners that form a constitute are in construction with one another. The meaning of a constitute will in some sense include the meaning of its ICs, but in addition gains something from the very fact that its ICs occur in construction with each other: the semantic relation between the ICs must be taken into consideration. It should be possible to vary one IC of a constitute at a time, substituting different morpheme sequences while holding constant the other IC(s) AND preserving as nearly as possible the original semantic relation between ICs. A construction may be thought of as a pattern of two (or more) classes of separately substitutable ICs bearing approximately

the same semantic relation to each other. E.g. *He left* exemplifies a pattern of two classes, nominal expression and verbal expression, which function as subject and predicate poles in a semantic relation that may be called 'actor performs action'.[11]

The basic problem of IC analysis is that of knowing how to segment utterances such that the constituents of various sizes may usefully be assigned to a relatively small number of constructions in a way that seems reasonable and natural. Although the present paper assumes a progress from utterance to morpheme, this does not imply that the opposite approach is not sometimes easier or more useful or more interesting.[12]

2. CRITERIA FOR IC CUTS. In the early period of IC analysis, linguists generally agreed that all and only the morphemic material in a constitute, be this the totality or only a portion of an utterance, should be cut into two and only two conjointly exhaustive ICs; only when the criteria, discussed below, failed to select either of two or more equally desirable binary cuts were multiple IC cuts permitted.[13] Given this overriding assumption, various criteria were advanced—explicitly or implicitly—as reasons for preferring this or that cut.

2.1. THE CRITERION OF INTERNAL COHESION. Internal cohesion means the degree to which a sequence functions as a unit; clearly, the pertinence of this criterion follows from the assumption that IC analysis is getting at something real and useful in the structure of language, and that ICs are not simply vacuous artifacts of analysis. We want, as Plato put it, to carve at the joints. Various investigators have defined and used the criterion of cohesion differently.

Wells (1947.83) states the criterion—his principle of expansion—as follows:

> We may roughly express the fact under discussion by saying that sometimes two sequences occur in the same environments even though they have different internal structures. When one of the sequences is at least as long as the other (contains at least as many morphemes) and is structurally diverse from it (does not belong to all the same sequence-classes as the other), we may call it an EXPANSION of that other sequence, and the other sequence itself we call a MODEL. If A is an expansion of B, B is a model of A. The leading idea of the theory of ICs here developed is to analyze each sequence, so far as possible, into parts which are expansions; these parts will be the constituents of the sequence.

. . . .

> Our general principle of IC-analysis is not only to view a sequence, when possible, as an expansion of a shorter sequence, but also to break it up into parts of which some or all are themselves expansions. Thus in our example it is valuable to view *The king of England opened Parliament* as an expansion of *John worked* because *the*

king of England is an expansion of *John* and *opened Parliament* is an expansion of *worked*. On this basis, we regard the ICs of *The king of England opened Parliament* as *the King of England* and *opened Parliament*.

It is recognized (Wells 1947.87) that cohesion is a relative matter:

> If two sequences belong to all the same sequence-classes,[14] then each is an ABSO-LUTE EQUIVALENT of the other, in the sense that each occurs in all the environments where the other occurs and nowhere else. However, it is rare, if it happens at all, that one sequence is an absolute equivalent of a sequence belonging to an entirely different sequence-class. On this account our interest centers in non-absolute expansions, and the problem is to find expansions that approximate as closely as possible to being absolute.

Note that Wells does not insist upon cutting into ICs that are expansions of single-morpheme or single-word models.

Nida, too,[15] emphasizes that this criterion—his principle of division on the basis of substitutability—is of primary importance. 'Divisions [into ICs] are made on the basis of the substitutability of larger units by smaller units belonging to the same or a different external distribution class.' And (1949.92) 'substitution by members of the same external distribution class is far more important than substitution by members of different classes, for in substitutions from the same class there is much greater likelihood of preserving the same meaningful relationships.'

Hockett invokes this criterion as one basis for IC cuts on the phonological stratum; cf. his discussion (1955.74) of the privileges of occurrence of Russian /ay ey oy/ as opposed to English /ay ey oy/.

Perhaps the simplest and clearest statement of the criterion of internal cohesion is that of Bazell:[16]

> By cohesion is meant the degree to which a group of units behaves, in the totality of possible environments, like a single unit. (The question may also be framed: how similar is the distribution of the higher-level unit to some lower-level unit?) Maximal cohesion is the virtual identity in functions of the group with a single unit.

Elsewhere Bazell emphasizes the importance of choosing ICs that are expansions of single-morpheme models: the criterion of 'distribution similar to that of indivisible units.'[17]

2.2. THE CRITERION OF INTERNAL DIVERSITY. Some writers explicitly state that one should prefer cuts yielding ICs each of which separately is substitutable by elements of maximally diverse internal structure. Let *in the ocean* be cut into *in* and *the ocean*: the second IC belongs to a class of substitutable sequences which has very high internal diversity—any nominal (e.g. *oceans of unplumbed depth whose waves lap every shore*); but the first belongs to a class of extremely low diversity, since for *in* may be substituted only other prepositions, sequences of prepositions (*out of*), or sequences like *in* or *on*. The importance of this criterion stems from our effort to reduce redundancy by setting up classes: the more inclusive and structurally diverse each class, the more redundancy has been handled at a single step.

Wells does not formally set up internal diversity as an independent criterion for cutting; rather (1947.87) he balances diversity against independence (see below), insisting that the best IC cuts yield chunks high in both diversity and independence:

> It is easy to define a focus-class embracing a large variety of sequence-classes but characterized by only a few environments; it is also easy to define one characterized by a great many environments in which all its members occur, but on the other hand poor in the number of diverse sequence-classes that it embraces. What is difficult, but far more important than either of the easy tasks, is to define focus-classes rich both in the number of environments characterizing them and at the same time in the diversity of sequence-classes that they embrace. Actor and action (or in older terminology subject and predicate) are such focus-classes.

Bloch, on the other hand, does separate this criterion: he seeks maximal heterogeneity (see note 14) in substitutability.

2.3. THE CRITERION OF INDEPENDENCE. The two preceding criteria concern the internal grammar of tentative ICs; of equal importance is their external grammar. We must seek 'ICs that will be as independent of each other in their distribution as possible' (Wells 1947.84), i.e. will occur in many different environments and constructions, with many different sorts of IC partners.

Hockett (1955.153) emphasizes the importance of such 'freedom of recombination' in phonological ICs.

Wells (1947.88), as noted above, lumps together this and the preceding criterion:

> This is the fundamental aim of IC-analysis: to analyze each utterance and each constitute into maximally independent sequences—sequences which, consistently preserving the same meaning, fit in the greatest number of environments [independence in my sense] and belong to focus-classes with the greatest possible variety of content [internal diversity in my sense].

Bloch (1953.44) uses the term 'ubiquity' in discussing this criterion:

> UBIQUITY—a wretched term, not only because it is not Greek like the rest, but also because it suggests more than I mean—is a matter of turning up in many different constructions, that is, with many different semantic relations to other constituents in the sequence.

Thus, Bloch gives primary emphasis to the criteria of internal diversity and independence when he states (1953.43–4): 'We try to divide [a sequence] so as to achieve tomes [= ICs] that belong to maximally heterogeneous and maximally ubiquitous tomemes' (= classes of ICs that are substitutable without altering the semantic relation to the IC that remains constant).

2.4. THE CRITERION OF JUNCTURE. 'By juncture is meant the degree to which the members of a group combine in a given series. (How close is this combination?) Juncture in the usual sense is a special instance of the relation' (Bazell 1951.4). The preceding three criteria were concerned with distributions and functions of sequences; the present criterion is a purely internal one, based on facts drawn from a lower stratum or lower tactical level.

Hockett is invoking the criterion of juncture when he states (1955.153): 'We base our cuts between ICs [of the phonological stratum] on the phonetic facts except where there is overwhelming reason (stemming from other criteria) not to.' Thus, in /imp/ we cut first between /i/ and /mp/ because /mp/ is a closer phonetic combination than /im/—or, to use Hockett's term (1955.151), has greater phonetic homogeneity. (Elsewhere Hockett uses the term 'internal cohesion' for what I call the criterion of juncture.)

Wells lays more stress on the importance of this criterion on the morphological stratum than any other writer: one of his primary points is his 'principle that word divisions should be respected' (1947.84). After a considerable discussion he concludes (1947.101–2):

Instead of proclaiming, therefore, that every word in every language must be a constituent of any sequence in which it occurs as a part, the most we may say is that every word should be so regarded unless it engenders a conflict or complication in the description of the language.

Some of the problems involved in combining this criterion with those of cohesion and independence are noted below.

2.5. CRITERIA OF SIMPLICITY. This is not the place for a discussion of the complexity of simplicity, but some prior notion of simplicity must underlie the choice and application of criteria such as those discussed here. Various appeals to simplicity are made or considered in discussions of IC analysis.

Wells, for example, considers (1947.85) that:

An argument might be based on economy or simplicity: the constituents of a sentence should be those units in terms of which the sentence is most easily described. [He continues in a footnote:] One particular version of simplicity which someone might propound but which must be rejected would call for the totality of analyses that requires the minimum number of sequence-classes to be defined.

Implicit assumption of some simplicity criterion is present in any appeal either to consistency of analysis or to patterning. As for the former, Wells states one important principle (1947.92):

A continuous sequence treated as a constituent in one environment should be treated as a constituent in any other environment where it occurs, UNLESS (1) there is some longer sequence of which it is both a part and a model (in other words, some endocentric expansion of it) and which is treated as a constituent or (2) it bears a different meaning.

But much more than this must be involved. One has only to attempt preliminary IC analysis of a language that one does not speak natively to realize the crushing truth of Wells's dictum that 'errors, as well as right analyses, compound each other' (1947.93). That is:

One IC-analysis involves others; its soundness is not tested until its most far-reaching effects in the system have been explored. Ultimately, what is accepted or rejected is not the analysis of a single sentence but what we may call the IC-SYSTEM of the language, an entire set or system of analyses, complete down to the ultimate constituents, of all the utterances of the language. Since every constitute is wholly composed of constituents, every proposal to regard such-and-such a sequence as a constituent entails that every other constituent of the sentence in which it occurs shall wholly include it or wholly exclude it or be wholly included in it. The analysis *the king of | England opened Parliament* is obviously excluded if *of England* is a constituent of that sentence; conversely, if *the king of | England opened Parliament* is the accepted analysis, it is impossible that *of England* should be a constituent. (Wells 1947.92–3.)

Precisely what principles of simplicity and consistency are involved in such webs of cross-implicating IC cuts?

Arguments from patterning are always dangerous and difficult, since they so often involve weighing different kinds of simplicity. Such arguments, too, are often so vague or amorphous as to be little more than pious hopes. Nida's Principle 3 (1949.92) states: 'Divisions [into ICs] should be supported by the total structure of the language.' More useful are Wells's discussion of associative groups and his patterning argument based on paradigms (1947.89–91).

2.6. PROVISION FOR MULTIPLE ICs. In discussing his Principle 3, that IC divisions should be as few as possible, Nida writes (1949.92):

Because we find from experience that linguistic structure tends to be binary ... we assume in analysis that a particular construction consists of two immediate constituents unless we cannot find substitutional patterns which will make such a division possible. There is, for example, no adequate manner in which we can describe the French adjective *rouge-blanc-bleu* 'red-white-blue' as anything but three immediate constituents. The same is true of the English *foot-pound-second* ... No two of these sets of constituents may be regarded as structurally prior to a third.

Similarly, Wells says (1947.103):

We propose to recognize multiple (three or more) ICs only under one definite condition. GIVEN A CONSTITUTE CONSISTING OF THREE CONTINUOUS SEQUENCES A, B, AND C, THEN, IF NO REASON CAN BE FOUND FOR ANALYZING IT AS AB|C RATHER THAN A|BC, OR AS A|BC RATHER THAN AB|C, IT IS TO BE ANALYZED INTO THREE CORRELATIVE ICs, A|B|C. Similarly, four ICs may be recognized when no analysis into two and no analysis into three ICs is recommended, and so on.

Wells considers English noun phrases of the type *A and B* possible examples of multiple ICs, and cuts *men and women* into three ICs corresponding to the word division. Nida (1949.92 n. 25) on the other hand would apparently cut into *men* and *and women*.

For more recent suggestions allowing multiple ICs under other circumstances see §4.4.

2.7. PROVISION FOR DISCONTINUOUS ICs. Wells writes (1947.104):

... if the admission of multiple and of discontinuous constituents were subject to no other restriction than yielding maximally independent constituents, IC-analysis would become a tremendously intricate affair. The possibilities requiring investigation would be enormously multiplied. A more orderly and manageable procedure is to extend the IC-system as far as possible on the basis of two continuous ICs for each constitute; and then to supplement this system and revise it where revision is called for by admitting the more complex kinds of analysis. In order to keep the revision at a minimum, we have proposed a restricting condition for multiple ICs, and we propose now the following for discontinuous ICs: A DISCONTINUOUS SEQUENCE IS A CONSTITUENT IF IN SOME ENVIRONMENT THE CORRESPONDING CONTINUOUS SEQUENCE OCCURS AS A CONSTITUENT IN A CONSTRUCTION SEMANTICALLY HARMONIOUS WITH THE CONSTRUCTIONS IN WHICH THE GIVEN DISCONTINUOUS SEQUENCE OCCURS. The phrase 'semantically harmonious' is left undefined, and will merely be elucidated by examples.

Thus, from [*It was a*] better [*movie*] *than I expected* may be extracted a discontinuous IC *better ... than I expected* (partner to *movie*) on the basis of [*The movie was*] *better than I expected*. Note that Wells's provision allows analysis of *the English king* into *English* plus *the ... king*, which supports a cut of *the king of England* into *the king* plus *of England* rather than into *the* plus *king of England*. Some provision for discontinuous ICs seems necessary —surely we want to extract a subject *you* from *What did you do?*—yet any such provision greatly complicates IC analysis. An extension to allow discontinuous ICs (and perhaps also that for multiple ICs) seems to change

IC analysis in kind and not just in degree; what would happen, for example, if discontinuous ICs were allowed on the phonological stratum?

2.8. PROVISION FOR CONSTRUCTIONAL HOMONYMY. The sequence *old men and women* is ambiguous: it seems that *old* may be an IC partner either of *men* alone or of *men and women*. Hence, Wells states (1947.96):

> ... when the same sequence has, in different occurrences, different meanings and therefore (provided that the meaning-difference cannot be ascribed to the morphemes taken separately) different constructions, it may have different IC-analyses. The IC-analysis of a sequence often reflects the semantic analysis of what the sequence means, but the meaning needs to be considered in making the analysis only when two occurrences of the same sequence (or of two sequences belonging to all the same sequence-types) have meanings incompatible with each other.

Here we are using the procedure of differentiation (cf. note 1) to resolve a case of IC ambiguity—i.e. ambiguity resulting from covert differences in IC structure which are inevitably accompanied by differences in construction (in Wells's sense). In other words, given an utterance and its total meaning, we must segment on both the morphological and sememic strata and attempt a correlation. Some fractions of the total meaning can be localized in individual morphemes; some can be localized in the co-occurrence of particular morphemes (i.e. in idioms such as *jack-in-the-pulpit* where the meaning of the sequence is different from the sum of the meanings of the constituent morphemes and their construction[s] and cannot be predicted from these meanings); as for the meaning that is as yet unlocalized, we use it as a guide to IC analysis, cutting in such a way as to have constructions in which the meaning-remainder may be said to be localized. Given an ambiguous sequence such that the difference between the two (or more) meanings cannot conveniently be localized in morphemes or idioms, we assume a difference in IC structure if that is possible. Obviously no such difference in IC structure is possible if that sequence contains only two morphemes (or lexemes): hence the independence of 'construction' from the other variables of syntax. Chinese *crau³ fan⁴* may mean 'to fry rice' and exemplify a verb-object construction, or as attribute-head construction it may mean 'fried rice'.[18]

3. PROBLEMS IN THE APPLICATION OF CRITERIA. Anyone who has ever attempted IC analysis is aware that the above criteria are often in conflict; hence, Wells does NOT propose to set up 'a mechanical procedure by which the linguist, starting with no other data than the corpus of all the utterances of the language and a knowledge of the morphemes contained in each one, may discover the correct [i.e. best] IC-system' (Wells 1947.93; cf. also 88 n. 9). More particularly, Bazell has delimited two problems of special interest, one involving conflict of criteria, the other fractionation of criteria.

3.1. Bazell points out (1951.4):

> In morphology the two relations [of cohesion and juncture; see citations in §2.1 and §2.4] do not tend to coincide. When therefore E. Nida (Syntax p. 55) analyses [sic] *au garçon* into constituents answering to the word-division, he does so on junctural criteria out of place in the generally cohesional system of immediate constituents. There is here a closer junctural relation between preposition and article, but a closer cohesional relation between article and noun. The word is a junctural, not a cohesional unit. The consequences have been drawn by one American scholar (Z. Harris), whose constituent-analyses cut through all word-divisions.

An investigation into the IC structure of West Middle Mongolian[19] showed that the criteria of cohesion and of juncture support one another in about half of the IC cuts; 'in the remaining cuts, however, (generally when an exocentric construction is involved) they flatly disagree' (Street 1957.72). Further, though cuts that respect word boundaries yield ICs which are more independent and internally diverse than those arrived at by emphasizing cohesion at the expense of juncture, it is the latter which make possible simpler overall grammatical statements. In other terms, the word in Mongolian is a unit of the phonological stratum which is simply irrelevant to syntax. Whereas in English syntax, morphemes like possessive $\sqrt{-'s}$ and possessing $\sqrt{-d}$ —as in *the man I met yesterday's hat* and *three-masted schooner*—are exceptional, in Mongolian such morphemes are the rule.

There is thus a temptation to delete juncture from the list of criteria for IC cuts, or at least to demote it to the status of a low-level subsidiary criterion. But of course there is no proof that any one variety of IC analysis—or any one model of syntactic analysis, for that matter—is necessarily the best for all languages.

3.2. For Bazell, cohesion is the sole primary criterion for IC cuts. But even (1953.65–7) this

> ... criterion of "distribution similar to that of indivisible units" may serve as an example of the way a criterion, perfectly clear in itself, splits up into several criteria upon application. For instance the following subcriteria are frequently in contradiction:
> (i) The frequency of substitutability by a single unit, and the frequency of substitutable units.
> In *large beast-s, large beast* is generally substitutable by many simple units, but the substitution cannot always be made: e.g. in *very large beast* a simple unit cannot be substituted. (This is the reason for the analysis *very large / beast*, for the substitution of a simple unit for *very large* is almost always possible.) On the other hand

beast-s is substitutable by very few simple units (e.g. *cattle*), but these few units are more generally substitutable.

(ii) The frequency of substitutability *by* a single unit, and the frequency of substitutability *for* a single unit.

The relation of the composite unit AB and the simple unit C may be one of *inclusive* distribution. One constituent-analysis might be favoured by the fact that the composite unit may be invariably replaceable by a simple unit, the other by the fact that the composite unit may invariably replace the simple unit, without the reverse in either case being true.

(iii) Frequency of substitutability by a single unit which is the same in each case, and frequency of substitutability by single units which differ according to context.

AB may commonly, though not invariably, be replaceable by C; or it may be invariably replaceable by *either* D *or* E. Conflict of criteria arises if AB stands in the former case for one potential constituent, and in the other case for another, in the same group.

(iv) It is also possible to hesitate over what may be described as substitution.

In *you paint the wall green*, *wall green* may obviously be replaced by *picture*. However the substitution cannot elsewhere usually be made. Far freer is the substitution of *wash* for *paint ... green*, if this can be described as a substitution. It is clear that the instruction 'substitute *wash* for *paint ... green*', in the sentence in question, is one which cannot be carried out with certainty of producing another possible utterance; the instruction is indeterminate at best. Further instructions must be given on the way in which such operations are to be carried out, and the fact that such instructions may be of a general kind (i.e. not applied *ad hoc* to the units in question) does not disguise the fact that the sense of substitution here is rather a marginal one.

(v) Finally hesitation may arise over whether the case is an appropriate one for the application of the criterion. For instance, instead of debating whether the relations of substitution favour one or the other division of *hot and cold*, when obviously none is favoured very strongly by this criterion, we may either choose quite a different criterion, or say that constituent analysis of the group as such is inappropriate. For example, *and* may be described as a 'marker', after which no question of constituents arises.

All these criteria naturally split up in their turn into as many more as one wishes. They cannot all be *explicitly* weighed against each other by the linguist; nor can the method of weighing against each other two incommensurable criteria be made explicit. Implicitly they all play their role.

This may be the place to list the chief types of marginality:

(i) A criterion susceptible of being satisfied in various degrees is only half-satisfied.

(ii) Two criteria are in contradiction (i–iii above).

(iii) The criterion is satisfied in some marginal sense (iv above).

(iv) The applicability of the criterion is dubious (v above).

3.3. In view of the complexity of IC analysis as discussed above, it is no wonder that different writers have divided similar structures in different ways.

The more theory-oriented writers usually state which of the above cri-

teria they intend to use, and sometimes imply a hierarchy of application.
Wells apparently places about equal weight on internal cohesion, independence, internal diversity, and juncture; Bloch (1953) stresses independence
and internal diversity; Bazell (1953.65) uses internal cohesion as the 'sole
primary criterion'; Street (1957) uses first internal cohesion, then independence, then internal diversity; Hockett, in phonology (1955.153), uses
first juncture, then internal cohesion and independence. Such differences
among analysts necessarily result in the making of different IC cuts. For
example, Bazell (1953.65) cuts (*John*) *opened the front door* into *open ... the
front door* and *-ed*—a cut not specifically discussed by Wells but contrary
to his general system. (This discontinuous IC, however, is permitted by the
proviso of §2.7.) Similarly Harris (1951.279) cuts:

    (2)   (5)   (4)   (3) (1)   (3)   (2)

My || most ||||| recent |||| plays|||-s | close||| down || +ed; but Chatman
(1955.381) objects that 'even a superficial glance at the formulation will
show a sharp contrast with the IC analysis as suggested by Bloomfield and
all other students:

    (2)   (4)   (3)   (5) (1) (3) (2)

My || most |||| recent || play||||||-s | clos|||ed || down.'

On the other hand, many writers who use IC analysis are interested in it
as a practical tool rather than as a problem in theory; most typically they
analyze without specifically defending or explaining individual cuts.
Francis, for example, cuts the predicate of (*my neighbor*) *painted his house
green* into *painted* and *his house green*, and that of (*the clerk*) *sold me the
shirt* into *sold* and *me the shirt*;[20] one wonders what construction is exempli-
fied by *me | the shirt*. Further, Francis (page 310) cuts *a fish out of water*
into *a fish* and *out of water*, but just two pages later he cuts *the high birth-
rate in America today* into *the* plus everything else; the former analysis
agrees with Roberts' principle that in 'noun clusters' one first cuts off
modifiers to the right of the head noun, and only later those to the left.[21]
(Note that Wells first [1947.89] cuts *the king of England* into *the* plus *king
of England*, but later [1947.106] says that a cut of *the king* plus *of England*
'after all seems to be the analysis favored by common sense.') In general,
however, those who write practical textbooks for English classes have dif-
fered less widely among themselves as to their IC cuts than have linguists
with a more theoretical orientation: the former could simply superimpose
the idea of IC analysis upon the ready-made and useful concepts of traditional grammar,[22] while the latter never ceased to be disturbed by the sorts
of syntactic problems that gave rise to transformational grammar.

4. MODIFICATIONS OF IC THEORY. We may now examine some of the modifications of basic IC theory that have been suggested from time to time by
various linguists.

4.1. MARKERS. It has often been suggested that under certain circumstances a constitute might be cut into ICs that are not conjointly exhaustive (cf. §2.)—i.e. some morphemic material of a constitute might be excluded from either (or any) IC. Hockett, for example, states (1954.214): 'Occasionally it is convenient to regard a morpheme not as participating in any construction, but rather as a MARKER of the construction in which nearby forms stand.' It may be desirable to consider *men and women* to consist of two ICs, *men* and *women*, with *and* taken as such a marker.

A set of conditions which would allow the interpretation in this case would have to be along the following lines: there is a form ABC consisting of three smaller forms, where (1) one of the smaller forms, say B (it would not have to be the one in the middle) is a single morpheme; (2) the remaining two, A and C, are structurally similar to each other (in some appropriate sense) but not to B; (3) there is no evidence forcing either an interpretation as A | BC or as AB | C (Hockett 1954.215).

For passing reference by Bazell to the possible usefulness of markers, see the passage cited in §3.2.

A similar but broader conception is that of Pittman, who speaks of 'overt valences ... carried' by specific morphemes:

It is possible to conceive of the relation between two immediate constituents as a sort of link, or bond, between the constituents. This bond [is] called a 'syntagmatic relation' by Hjelmslev ... It is possible to conceive of the syntagmatic relations between the terminals ... [of *very* → → *fine, man* ← → *hour, John* → ← *ran*] as a sort of 'bond' or 'valence' connecting the terminals.

.   .   .   .

In most cases it is probably more difficult to identify valences than morphemes, since the former are frequently covert features whose identity may be determined only by observing which constituents and classes are presupposed by certain other constituents and classes. Certain phonological sequences, however, which have usually been described as morphemes, might perhaps be more neatly described as 'overt valences'. These overt valences may appear to be very similar to morphemes, or, indeed, they may be 'carried' by specific morphemes. Possible examples of this might be the unit *to* in English infinitive expressions and the suffix -*r* in Spanish infinitives. The English auxiliary 'do' in expressions such as *I do not know* is another likely example.

Elements such as these do not have a morphemic status, in the conventional sense of our term 'morpheme', but serve rather as simple overt valences connecting the stem of the infinitive with the verb which introduces it.

.   .   .   .

It is not necessary that the valence-carrying morpheme appear *between* the two constituents which it unites. The Latin conjunction -*que* is an example of one which does not.[23]

Unfortunately Pittman's discussion is very brief and leaves a number of points unclear; but clearly the concept of valence allows more elements to be omitted from ICs than does Hockett's condition cited above.[24]

4.2. OVERLAPPING ICs. In the preceding section it was suggested that some morphemic material of a constitute might be excluded from the ICs of this constitute; this implies the converse, that some morphemic material of a constitute might be assigned simultaneously to both ICs. To the best of my knowledge no one has ever followed up this possibility in syntactic cuts. In phonology, however, Hockett (1955.152) does make use of such a SHARED CONSTITUENT or PIVOT; e.g. he assigns the /l/ of *believe* to both syllables, thus /bi(l)/ and /(l)iyv/.

It seems likely that overlapping ICs might at times be very useful in cutting on the morphological stratum as well as on the phonological; there is even the possibility of inclusion of one IC within another, or of total overlap. For example, Cyrillic Khalkha Mongolian *tiim bol* 'in that case' (lit. 'if it be so') might be cut into *tiim bol* 'be so' (consisting of *tiim* 'so, that way' plus *bol* 'to be, become') plus *bol* 'if'; the expected form *bolbol* 'if it be' is usually shortened to *bol* by haplology,[25] and the concept of overlapping ICs permits descriptive resolution of this process. (If on the other hand IC analysis is applied to a purely morphemic transcription, rather than to a morphophonemic one, this haplologized form can be treated as a portmanteau morph, and the present solution is unnecessary.) Similarly, the ICs of [*He has*] *no special knowledge of, or interest in mathematics* might be taken as *no special knowledge of mathematics* and *no interest in mathematics*, with *or* as a marker.

4.3. DOUBLE IC STRUCTURE. I have twice[26] ventured a more extreme suggestion (originally as a device of dissertational desperation, and later only with grave reservations): that some constitutes may be thought of as having, in part, double IC structure, i.e. should be cut into ICs in two different ways. One of the cuts typically results in two ICs each of which is neither an ultimate constituent (morpheme or lexeme) nor a constitute. In Mongolian, for example, certain morpheme sequences that do not form a constitute may be expanded by the addition of a parallel morpheme sequence. Given a sequence *ABC* with the constituents *A–BC* and *B–C*, the 'accidental' collocation *AB* may be expanded to produce a sequence *ABabC* with the ICs *Aa–BbC*, *A–a*, *Bb–C*, *B–b*, but also apparently *AB–ab*, where, however, *A* is not in construction with *B*, nor *a* with *b*. E.g.:

qorcin	qor	bawurcin	ayaqa saba	kebteüle taulju odtuqay.
A	B	a	b	C

'Let the quiver-bearers hand over [their] quivers to the night-watch, and the cooks [their] bowls and cups' (Street 1957.50). Element *C* is 'let ... hand over to the night-watch'; A and a are subjects (of BbC) 'the quiver-bearers' and 'the cooks'; B and b are objects (of C) 'quiver[s]' and 'bowl[s and] cup[s]'. Either ABC or abC would be a perfectly good sentence. $AaBbC$ is also a sentence, meaning 'Let the quiver-bearers and cooks hand over [their] quivers, bowls, and cups to the night-watch'; so that the interlocking order of subjects and objects adds the meaning 'respectively'. The interlocking order (Street 1957.50) indicates an added coordinate construction $AB-ab$ simultaneous with the coordinate structures $A-a$ and $B-b$.

A similar analysis might be used for English

$$\underline{\underline{\text{John}} \quad \underline{\text{got}} \quad \underline{\text{a book}} \quad \underline{\text{from his aunt}}}$$
$$\text{X} \qquad \text{C} \qquad \text{A} \qquad \quad \text{B}$$

which is expandable into

$$\underline{\underline{\text{John}} \ \underline{\text{got}} \ \underline{\text{a book}} \ \underline{\text{from his aunt}} \ \underline{\text{and}} \ \underline{\text{a bicycle}} \ \underline{\text{from his parents}}.}$$
$$\text{X} \quad \text{C} \quad \text{A} \qquad \text{B} \qquad \quad \text{D} \qquad a \qquad \quad b$$

The shorter sentence presumably has the ICs $X–CAB$, $CA–B$, and $C–A$ with the sequence AB as an accidental collocation. Yet in the longer sentence AB is expanded into $AB^{D}ab$, i.e. $AB–ab$ with D as a marker. In the longer sentence, then, we have the ICs $X–CABDab$, $CAa–Bb$, $C–Aa$, $A–a$, $B–b$, and simultaneously $AB^{D}ab$ (or if overlapping ICs are permitted, $X–CABDab$, $CADa–BDb$, $C–ADa$, $A^{D}a$, $B^{D}b$, and simultaneously $AB^{D}ab$). Similar analyses might be made of sentences such as:

> *Wait till the lights are out and the people asleep.*
> *He painted the wall green and the woodwork white.*
> *He gave me a book and my brother a bicycle.*

And with chiasmus:

> *I'll give you three dollars for all the books but for one of them no more than fifty cents.*

While such double analyses could be extended to cover other structures usually considered the results of transformations, it is doubtful whether the resulting statements would be either particularly efficient or intuitively satisfying. At any rate, if overlapping ICs are permitted (and can somehow be kept under control) such double analyses are unnecessary, since element C in the English example may simply be allowed to be in construction with both AB and ab; in traditional terms a second *got* is understood in *John got a book from his aunt and (got) a bicycle from his parents*.[27]

Hockett[28] claims that 'a grammar that makes use of both constructions and of not more than a finite number of transformations can be converted into a pure constructional grammar', and by way of illustration sets up different symbols for the subject of an active clause on the one hand, and on the other for the subject of a sentence which constitutes 'a passive transformation of an active clause in which what precedes [i.e. the element usually taken as subject] would have been the object.' It is not clear just what Hockett intended here; his statements might possibly be interpreted as implying double IC structure, i.e. that the subject of a passive is simultaneously the object of the bare verb or of some other part of the predicate.

4.4. NONBINARY ANALYSIS. The basic principle of binary cuts in IC analysis has often been questioned. E.g. Bazell writes (1953.5):

> The idea of an overwhelmingly predominating binary structure of immediate constituents is again largely illusory. Even the most common English utterance-type does not fit into this view. In e.g. *John started* the primary criterion of substitution [i.e. cohesion] does not yield any analysis, since neither *John start-* nor *start-ed* can be replaced by a monomorphemic constituent. For this reason it is usual to follow the word-division; but this is a very different sort of criterion. And it is not in the least surprising that if one applies one criterion after another in a fixed hierarchical order, until one comes to the first criterion that yields a binary division, one will be able to make this division sooner or later; though a different order of criteria would have yielded a different result. The success of this method is a tribute, not to the importance of the binary character of the syntagm, but simply to the *acharnement* with which the linguists seek to split up utterance-segments into two.

Longacre argues that only 'some linguistic structures are layered, while others are ordered like beads on a string',[29] i.e. that we should recognize hierarchical structure where it exists, but not force it upon all constitutes. He raises the objections (1) that 'the requirement that we make successive dichotomous cuts (a requirement waived only under very special conditions) yields constructions of which some are unquestionably relevant to the structure in hand, but others are much less relevant' and (2) that 'there is no system in regard to the rank of various cuts' (1960.66–7). His proposed string-constituent analysis assumes 'that a hierarchy of such units as word, phrase, clause, and sentence characterizes language' (1960.68) (though each of these terms must be defined with reference to the language at hand), and attempts to cut a sentence into clauses at one step, clauses into phrases at the next, phrases into words at the next. (Note the implicit junctural criterion: every word is a constituent [1960.69].) Thus, the sentence *The slow, lumbering covered wagon pulled the pioneer's family across the prairie just yesterday but today giant trailer trucks and low-slung modern cars stream along broad highways where once he blazed the trail* is cut (1960.65–9) first into two clauses between *yesterday* and *but*. The first clause is then cut into five phrases: *the slow lumbering covered wagon, pulled, the pioneer's family, across the prairie,* and *just yesterday.* (It is the binary cut of this clause into subject and predicate that Longacre considers (1960.66) 'perhaps not so relevant and possibly even a trifle forced in regard to the "construction" ' left as the predicate.) Each of the phrases is then cut into words (corresponding to the orthography): *the slow ... wagon* is cut into five ICs, while *pulled* remains (or is cut into?) one; *the pioneer's family* is cut into three, etc. Further cuts will separate inflectional morphemes from stems, and so on.

The criteria used for cuts such as those proposed by Longacre are more complex than those discussed in §2.; to explain them would involve a more detailed exposition of Pike's tagmemic theory than space here permits. The fact that 'a string on a given level may include another string on the same or on a different level'—either higher or lower (1960.85–6)—seems to destroy much of the apparent neatness of Longacre's scheme.

For various earlier systems which permitted a constitute to consist of a single IC, see Wells 1947.102 (and esp. nn. 37–8).

Harris' theory of string analysis[30] in effect also argues for multiple as opposed to binary IC cuts.[31]

String analysis characterizes the sentences of a language as follows: Each sentence consists of one elementary sentence (its center), plus zero or more elementary adjuncts, i.e. word-sequences of particular structure which are not themselves sentences and which are adjoined immediately to the right or to the left of an elementary sentence or adjunct, or of a stated segment of an elementary sentence or adjunct, or of any one of these with adjuncts adjoined to it. An elementary sentence or adjunct is a string of words, the words (or particular sequences of them) being its successive segments. Each word is assigned (on the basis of its affixes or its position in elementary sentences and adjuncts) to one or more word categories (rarely, word-sequence categories). Hence, we can replace each word of a string by the symbol of its category, thus obtaining a string of category-symbols (called a string formula) as a representation of the word-string in question. The term "string" will be used both for word-strings and for string formulas, depending on the subject under discussion.

For example, in the sentence
Today, automatic trucks from the factory which we just visited carry coal up the sharp incline:
trucks carry coal is the elementary sentence
today, is an adjunct to the left of the elementary sentence
automatic is an adjunct to the left of *trucks*
from the factory is an adjunct to the right of *trucks*
which we visited is an adjunct to the right of *factory*
just is an adjunct to the left of *visited* [a note here discusses the ambiguity]
up the incline is an adjunct to the right of *carry*
sharp is an adjunct to the left of *incline.*
... it is possible to decompose each sentence into elementary strings which combine (to form a sentence) in accordance with specified rules. If in a given sentence we find a sequence of words which cannot be assigned to any known string formula

106 J. C. Street

occurring in it in accordance with some known rule, then a new string or rule of occurrence has to be set up. The intention is that a few classes of strings, with simple rules describing how they occur in relation to each other, will suffice to characterize all sentences of the language (Harris 1962. 9–10).

The criteria for decomposition of sentences involve Harris' total theory of syntax, and a discussion of them is beyond the scope of the present paper. A careful reading of Harris' *String analysis of sentence structure* (as of his earlier works) will amply reward any reader involved in practical linguistic analysis.

4.5. USE OF TRANSITIONAL PROBABILITIES. In a review of Shannon and Weaver's *The mathematical theory of communication*, Hockett suggests that information theory might offer a criterion for IC analysis:[32]

At various points in an utterance in the course of transmission, say at the ends of successive morphemes, the degree of indeterminacy as to what may come next can in theory be computed. The indeterminacy is greater if the number of possible next morphemes is greater; with a given number the indeterminacy is greater if the probabilities are nearly equal, less if they diverge widely from equality. Now generally in current practice, and universally in a theoretically possible optimum procedure, a linguist makes his primary cut of a composite form at that point where the indeterminacy is greatest. The form *red hats* (we ignore supersegmental features) consists of three morphemes, with a cut between *red* and *hat* and another between *hat* and *-s*. It would seem that the indeterminacy after *red* is greater than that after *red hat*; certainly it is if we regard the singular form *hat* as involving a morpheme of zero shape 'singular', since in that case there is only a small handful of morphemes which can immediately follow *red hat-*: this singular morpheme, or *-s* or *-ed* (*red-hatted*), or perhaps one or two others. Some forms, it may be, are not actually so cut, because the pressure of their similarity to large numbers of forms where the cutting is unambiguous may lead us to go counter to this first and fundamental criterion. Thus there is probably greater indeterminacy after the *hermetic-* of *hermetically sealed* than there is after the whole first word, but we would all choose to cut first between the words.

This suggestion is picked up and further exemplified by Chatman (1955, esp. 382–5), though without reference to Hockett's last point—the significance of which is reflected in Harris' distinction[33] between predecessor counts and successor counts. However, while Hockett considers transitional probabilities in terms of morphemes, Chatman rather attempts the more feasible task of counting the number of word classes that could follow each morpheme of a sequence; both Hockett and Chatman seem to have been interested in the theoretical pertinence of transitional probabilities to IC analysis primarily because these seemed to support the junctural criterion for IC cuts as opposed to that of internal cohesion.

As computers have become more popular and more accessible, a number of attempts have been made to produce programs for automatic parsing of sentences.[34] An evaluation of such programs is beyond my competence, but one brief comment is perhaps in order. The phrase-analyses produced by a program depend directly on the number and type of form classes in terms of which counts are made. Any decision on what form classes to count depends on one's total theory of grammar: a particular concept of form class is interdependent with some specific concept of construction, IC, rewrite rule, or the like. Hence, a parsing program does not discover grammatical structure, but rather tests the usefulness of a particular grammatical theory. It is not surprising to find that the branching tree diagrams produced by some programs for English differ strikingly from those preferred by more traditional IC theory, and also from those generated by transformational grammar.

4.6. PHRASE-STRUCTURE GRAMMAR. Most of the sources cited so far have assumed an attempt to segment utterances, and have focused on possible criteria for making cuts or on criteria for deciding which of two possible cuts is preferable. Generative grammar in general, and transformational grammar in particular, of course, assume rather an attempt to write rules to generate sentences of a language over which one has native-like control. The earliest rules of the syntactic component of a transformational grammar are rules that generate the underlying constituent structure of sequences (not yet sentences) to which optional and obligatory transformations may be applied. Constituent-structure rules presuppose the descriptive model that has been called phrase-structure grammar; the transformational parts of a transformational grammar add rules of much greater generative power than phrase-structure grammar rules. Phrase-structure grammar is generative, while IC analysis, as discussed above, is analytic. Nonetheless it has been claimed that

... the so-called theory of phrase structure, which was developed in precise formal terms only within the framework of generative grammar, correctly represents the underlying conception of grammatical description prevalent in modern linguistics generally, especially in modern American linguistics (Postal 1964.v in note 31).

If this is so, we may turn phrase structure upside down, looking at it from the analytical point of view rather than from the generative, and compare it with other systems of IC analysis. We find the following:

1. Phrase-structure grammar typically uses branching tree diagrams to represent structure in place of the various box diagrams, parenthesizations, or purely verbal statements found in discussions of IC structure. Obviously this difference is trivial.

2. The trees of phrase-structure grammar are always labeled, i.e. at least every node is marked as, for example, NP (noun phrase), N (noun), Aux

(auxiliary), etc. In the various models of grammatical description that use IC analysis, on the other hand, information such as that represented by the labels of labeled trees is often handled by separate statements about form classes and constructions rather than by inclusion in statements about ICs. Despite the fact that in a preliminary syntactic analysis decisions about IC cuts are interdependent with decisions on form classes and constructions, and despite the fact that most statements in full descriptive grammars present simultaneously information about ICs, constructions, and form classes, it remains nonetheless true that many theoretical discussions and partial descriptions treat IC structures in such a way as to make them equivalent to unlabeled trees.

3. There is no insistence on binary structure in phrase-structure grammar. In effect, a constitute may consist of one, two, or more than two ICs.

4. Phrase-structure grammar does not permit discontinous ICs; any discontinuity is taken to be the result of a transformation—usually one involving permutation, but possibly also adjunction or substitution (cf. Postal 1964.67 and 94 n. 115). The same is true of markers, which in most or all cases are 'transformationally introduced constants and have no phrase structure origin' (Postal 1964.92 n. 97). Likewise, any presumed case of overlapping ICs or double IC structure can be better handled by a transformation involving deletion or by a generalized transformation.

5. No less important: provision for constructional homonymy is probably not needed within the constituent structure part of a transformational grammar,[35] although phrase-structure grammar in its most general terms does not forbid such constructional homonymy (cf. Postal 1964.22 diagrams 6 and 7).

In light of these characteristics of phrase-structure grammar, it is self-evident that this form of grammar alone is inadequate for the description of any large part of a language. Transformational grammar adds the more powerful transformational rules in a particular way, while the grammatical theories of Wells, Bloch, Hockett, Harris, Pike, et al. add various other descriptive devices such as provisions for discontinuous constituents, markers, etc. Postal's claim that the syntactic conception of these scholars is 'essentially equivalent' to phrase-structure grammar is thus—at best—an overstatement.

4.7. STRATIFICATIONAL GRAMMAR. Lamb's theory of stratificational grammar is still in the process of development. In an early presentation of his ideas Lamb (1962.20–6) included a section on tactics which dealt with constructions and ICs, but since this section introduces a large number of special symbols, definitions, and operational rules that will certainly be revised, it is not worthwhile to go into details here.

Later presentations[36] clearly indicate that stratificational grammar is generative rather than analytic; cf. the statement that 'given a properly formulated set of representational rules, it is always possible to convert correctly to the next lower stratum but not vice-versa' (Lamb, 'The sememic approach ...' 1964.63). This, and the complex relations assumed by Lamb between the sememic and lexemic strata (the latter equivalent to part of what above was called the morphological stratum), make it unclear what part—if any—IC analysis and IC structure will eventually play in stratificational grammar. However, it seems inevitable that this grammatical model will at the very least suggest major modifications in IC theory.

5. The application of IC analysis. In light of the multiple and often conflicting criteria for IC analysis, and the various alternative views of IC structure discussed above, what advice can a teacher of linguistics give to the student who is tackling his first syntactic analysis of a corpus of utterances in a little-known language? To the questions 'How do you do IC analysis?' and 'What is an IC?' there is no simple answer; but several points may offer some clarification.

1. No one has ever succeeded in giving a rigorous definition of an IC, i.e. a statement of the sufficient and necessary conditions for IC-hood such as to enable one who lacks the native-speaker's intuitions in a particular language to identify positive and negative instances of ICs in that language.

2. What IC cuts one will make depends in large measure on one's concept of construction. Every choice between IC cuts implies some shift (though perhaps minimal) of grammatical statements from one part of the grammar-to-be to another; only an unwavering theory of construction will produce cuts conducive to a consistent grammar without unnecessary and intrusive complications.

3. Before attempting cuts, the student must do two things: first, he must decide what theory of syntax to follow and in particular what concept of construction to use; second, he must learn BY EXAMPLE what ICs are and are not under that particular theory. It does not matter whether he prefers Pike's tagmemic theory, Hockett's constructional grammar, Harris' string analysis, or any other analogous theory; but he must make a choice and stick to it at least until his first rough analysis is complete. He must be well acquainted with the books and articles which expound the theory—or, better still, hear the theory explained by its author or one of the latter's disciples.[37] Having understood some particular concept of construction, form class, etc. (whatever these may be called in the particular theory), the student should then examine in some detail two or three actual grammars, complete or partial, that exemplify the theory. Admittedly, a student on the verge of writing a grammar of Menominee, say, may find it hard to

force himself to study someone else's grammatical sketch of Nahuatl or
Chinese, but such study will help the student to learn (by largely uncon-
scious processes) what ICs are like under a given theory of construction.

4. Next the student must simply dive into the analysis and make cuts
as best he can. In all probability a large number of cuts will be obvious;
this is so partly because the particular syntactic theory he is using has built
into it certain decisions on where to cut.

5. One or two major problems may well arise right at the start: in the
third or fourth sentence, perhaps, two cuts are possible, both of which look
good according to the syntactic theory being used. In this case one should
make both cuts, and separately follow through the implications of each for
the internal structure of the grammar-to-be. Here a careful consideration of
possible criteria for IC cuts may be helpful. In an analysis of Mongolian,
for example, the problem early arose whether to cut *bi neke-sü* 'I'll pursue
[them]' (lit. 'I pursue-will') into *bi | neke-sü* or *bi neke-|-sü* (Street 1957.
72–3). The former (junctural) cut forces one to repeat a considerable number of grammatical statements at three different points in the resulting
grammar. Hence the second (cohesional) cut is preferable.

6. If such major problems do not arise early, the analyst will probably
face only minor problems: cases where the language doesn't really seem to
care much which way you cut. Probably the use of subcriteria will permit
some sort of consistency in such cases. One should avoid the choice of a cut
that seems purely arbitrary; further investigation will usually turn up some
fact that favors one cut over the other.

7. In the long run the only absolute requirement in preliminary analysis
is consistency. As long as obviously conflicting cuts are avoided, some
pattern will emerge.

8. At some point the point of diminishing returns will be reached: the
consideration of new utterances will rarely result in new problems of cutting,
and hence one may conclude that nearly all of the constructions of the language have been dealt with. This is the time for summarizing and stock-
taking. With the main outlines of the total grammar kept in mind, it is
well to go back and consider all the major and problematic decisions on IC
cuts in light of this total pattern. Certain alternations may be required; it
may even seem necessary to adjust the overall syntactic theory that has
been used as a frame of reference.

9. A tentative grammar of the language may now be committed to paper.
This grammar will certainly be less than fully satisfactory to its writer: it
will have involved some generalization based on inadequate evidence, it
will 'generate' many nonoccurring utterances (i.e. have poor negative fit),
it may even, in places, show that expediency has forced abandonment of
the canons of linguistic theory. But all grammars leak; every grammar is in

need of revision; no grammar yet written describes—much less explains—all the appropriate facts about the structure of any language. The linguist must be grateful for small favors: ANY new regularity he can discover in a language represents a step in the right direction.

10. The theory of transformational grammar perhaps yields a deeper understanding of the multifarious aspects of language behavior than any other theory. Yet transformational grammar is not recommended as the basic frame of reference for the first grammar of a little-known language. Transformational grammar aims at an explanation of all the assorted intuitions of the native speaker of the language, and these intuitions cannot be explained by one who does not himself possess them. Any generative grammar works from the top down as it were, from sentence to phone, while an analytical grammar works from the bottom up. The native speaker has gotten on top of his language during the childhood process of language-learning; the linguist who is not a native speaker can get to the top of it only by beginning to learn to speak the language and simultaneously writing an analytic grammar. After completing such a grammar and gaining at least some speaking ability, the linguist will be able to recast his grammatical understanding into a transformational mold. But if transformational grammar is used from the very start, an analyst is liable to be constantly twisting the language's arm and forcing upon it the structure of his own native language.

This does not mean, however, that the student cannot make use of the insights of transformational grammar in his fieldwork and preliminary analysis; the more he knows about ANY aspect of linguistic theory the better job he will do. Remembering, for example, that any need for discontinuous ICs, markers, overlapping ICs, double IC structure, or constructional homonymy indicates the presence of a transformation, he may be able to produce a more consistent and insightful analysis in terms of analytic grammar, and his data will be so collected and organized that, later on if he wishes, he can more easily progress to a generative study of the language at hand.

NOTES

1   'Segmentation involves cutting strings of units of a stratum (e.g. strings of phonemes) into substrings which are representations of higher-stratum units (e.g. morphemes). Differentiation involves distinguishing two or more higher-stratum units (e.g. past participle, past tense) represented in the same lower-stratum segment (e.g. -ed). And grouping involves the recognition that two or more differentiated segments of the lower stratum (e.g. -ed, -en) represent a single unit of the higher stratum (e.g. past participle). These three operations

cannot be performed in isolation. In practice, they are performed together.'
Sydney M. Lamb, *Outline of stratificational grammar* 6 (Berkeley, 1962).

2 Cf. Charles F. Hockett, *A manual of phonology* (Indiana Univ. publications in anthropology and linguistics, mem. 11; *International journal of American linguistics* 21:4:pt. 1) 43 (Bloomington, 1955).

3 Cf. Sydney M. Lamb, 'The sememic approach to structural semantics', in *Transcultural studies in cognition* (special publication of *American anthropologist* 66:3:pt. 2) 58 (1964).

4 Cf. E. R. Gammon, 'On representing syntactic structure', *Language* 39.369–97, esp. 377–8 (1963).

5 Bernard Bloch, 'Linguistic structure and linguistic analysis', *Monograph series on languages and linguistics* 4.43, Georgetown University Institute of Languages and Linguistics (Washington, D.C., 1953). The works referred to are listed in notes 6, 7, and 8.

6 Rulon S. Wells, 'Immediate constituents', *Lg.* 23.81–117 (1947) [reprinted in *Readings in linguistics* 186–207 Washington, D.C., 1957].

7 Leonard Bloomfield, *Language* (New York, 1933).

8 Kenneth Pike, 'Taxemes and immediate constituents', *Lg.* 19.65–82 (1943).

9 Cf. Kenneth L. Pike and Eunice V. Pike, 'Immediate constituents of Mazatec syllables', *IJAL* 13.78–91 (1947) and Hockett (1955).

10 Seymour Chatman, 'Immediate constituents and expansion analysis', *Word* 11.380 (1955), objects that Harris' utterance-to-morpheme procedures are not equivalent to IC analysis; but this objection is not valid if within IC analysis we allow as much latitude for choice and ranking of criteria as is here suggested.

11 The term 'construction' has been used in widely differing meanings, and is often ambiguously used in the work of a single writer. In many cases the decision on where to make IC cuts will depend at least partly on one's definition of (or conception of) construction. See §5.

12 Cf. Zellig S. Harris, 'From morpheme to utterance', *Lg.* 22.161–83 (1946) [reprinted in *Readings in linguistics* 142–53], and Harris, *Methods in structural linguistics* 262–98, esp. 278–80 (Chicago, 1951).

13 This followed Bloch's adage to the effect that whenever no convincing reason can be advanced for preferring either of two equally possible analyses, one abandons both and finds some third alternative.

14 Cf. Wells 1947.82: 'Given a [morpheme] sequence S, a sequence-class to which S belongs is defined as the class of all sequences whose first morpheme belongs to the same morpheme-class as the first morpheme of S, whose second morpheme belongs to the same morpheme-class as the second morpheme of S, and so on; it follows that all members of a given sequence-class contain the same number of morphemes.' Bloch's (1953.44) term and definition are perhaps more usable: Two sequences 'are HOMOGENEOUS if they contain the same number of morphemes and if every morpheme of one shares membership in at least one morpheme class with the corresponding morpheme of the other. To the extent that this requirement is not met the tomes [= constituents] are HETEROGENEOUS.'

15 Eugene A. Nida, *Morphology: The descriptive analysis of words*[2] 91 (Ann Arbor, 1949).

16 C. E. Bazell, 'Structural notes', *Istanbul edebiyat fakültesi ingilizce zümresi dergisi* 2.3–4 (Istanbul, 1951).
17 C. E. Bazell, *Linguistic form* 65 (Istanbul, 1953).
18 Charles F. Hockett, 'Two models of grammatical description', *Word* 10.222 (1954). Wells's example (1947.97) of *lady-killer* in this connection is perhaps not a good one, since one might allow the cut *lady | killer* for the meaning 'killer who is a lady', but *lady kill|er* for 'one who kills (metaphorical sense) ladies'. However, not all apparently homonymous constructions can be taken care of by differing IC cuts; cf. '[*the ship*] *is new, untried, lying in a river that lacks the tang of salt water, waiting for the men to man her*' Nicholas Monsarrat, *The cruel sea* 3 (New York, 1955). Here it seems unlikely that any difference in IC cuts could account for the ambiguity of the last seven words. Similarly *It's difficult to paint glass.*
19 John C. Street, *The language of the secret history of the Mongols* (American oriental series, vol. 42) esp. 72–3 (New Haven, 1957).
20 W. Nelson Francis, *The structure of American English* 329 (New York, 1958).
21 Paul Roberts, *Patterns of English* 117 (New York, 1956).
22 A noteworthy exception is James Sledd (*A short introduction to English grammar* 216–7 [Chicago, 1959]): 'Since the [IC] analyses which have so far been proposed differ widely among themselves and are often quite arbitrary, it has seemed best to make no direct statement about immediate constituents in this book.' Cf. the same writer's discussion of problems facing the contemporary writer of pedagogical grammars.
23 Richard Saunders Pittman, *A grammar of Telecingo (Morelos) Nahuatl* (Language dissertation, no. 50; *Lg.* suppl. 30:1:pt. 2) 6–8 (1954).
24 In his *A course in modern linguistics* (New York, 1958), Hockett uses the term 'marker' or 'pure marker' for elements excluded from ICs; his 'impure markers' —elements such as English prepositions—form one IC of a directive construction. Note, however, that English possessive *-'s* is called a marker (209 and cf. Fig. 17.6 on 153). This raises three points. (1) It suggests that Hockett's statement (209) that 'markers are defined as separate words' should be modified to read 'markers are defined as separate lexemes'. (2) It implies that Hockett does not use the criterion of juncture in IC cuts, for this criterion clearly favors a cut after the possessive. (3) The question remains what *-'s* is in *It's the king of England's*, and why such predicates do not favor cutting after the *-'s* and thus preclude the possibility of calling *-'s* a marker. It is clear that *-'s* is not a marker according to Hockett's set of conditions cited above; somehow Hockett must have broadened his concept of (pure) marker.
25 See John C. Street, *Khalkha structure* (Indiana Univ. Uralic and Altaic series, vol. 24) 231 (Bloomington, 1963). The forms here are transliterated from Cyrillic: use of the phonemic shapes would introduce messy morphophonemic problems.
26 Street 1957.50–1 and 1963.239–40. Unfortunately there is an error of statement in the latter discussion: the second clause of the second sentence on p. 240 should read: 'A is in construction with BB', ABB' with CC', B with B', and C with C', while simultaneously BC is in construction with B'C' although B is NOT in construction with C, nor B' with C'.'

27   This solution is obvious for English; it probably will not handle all the problems in Mongolian. Some Mongolian constructions still seem to require either double IC structure, or some sort of complex generalized transformation, or some other analytical tool outside the usual IC-construction-form-class kind of syntax.

28   Charles F. Hockett, 'Grammar for the hearer', in *The structure of language and its mathematical aspects*, R. Jakobson, ed. (*Proceedings of symposia in applied mathematics*, vol. 12) 231 (Providence, 1961).

29   Robert E. Longacre, 'String constituent analysis', *Lg.* 36.63 (1960).

30   Zellig S. Harris, *String analysis of sentence structure* (The Hague, 1962).

31   While Harris asserts that string analysis is essentially different from, and stronger than, constituent analysis (being intermediate between constituent analysis and transformational analysis), this claim has been disputed by Paul Postal, *Constituent structure: A study of contemporary models of syntactic description* 61–66 (Bloomington, 1964). It seems that the differences claimed by Harris rest on a rather narrow definition of constituent analysis which includes a particular theory of construction and particular analytic procedure. According to Postal (63–4): '... in PSG [= phrase-structure grammar] terms it is easy to see that Harris' distinction between 'constituent analysis' and 'adjunct analysis' really amounts to just a differentiation between those elements which occur in parentheses (or, in tagmemic terms, with a plus and a minus sign) from those which do not. Thus if there is a rule like:

$$R71 \quad A \rightarrow (B)C$$

then C is the characterizing category of the phrase type A and B is a left adjunct. In the case where R71 is a low order rule, C will be the characteristic word class of the phrase type A. Thus if a set of PSG rules is provided with conventions for using parentheses, as is necessary on quite other grounds, it is clear that the distinction drawn by Harris is automatically characterized.'

32   *Lg.* 29.87–8 (1953).

33   Zellig S. Harris, 'From phoneme to morpheme', *Lg.* 31.190–222 (1955).

34   E.g. Jane J. Robinson, *Preliminary codes and rules for the automatic parsing of English*, Memorandum RM-3339-PR; The Rand Corporation (Santa Monica, Calif., 1962).

35   Cf. Noam Chomsky, *Syntactic structures* 87 n. 2 (The Hague, 1957).

36   Sydney M. Lamb, 'On alternation, transformation, realization, and stratification', *Monograph series on languages and linguistics* 17.105–22, Georgetown University Institute of Languages and Linguistics (Washington, D.C., 1964); and Lamb, 'The sememic approach ...' (1964).

37   Which theory a student picks will often be the result of historical and geographical accidents rather than of conscious choice. What is important is not what theory he chooses, but that he really understand SOME theory and be able to apply it to actual problems.

11

A MODEL FOR FRENCH SYNTACTIC DESCRIPTION

Ann Tukey

Description of syntax has generally been the afterthought of analyses; as the third of the 'phonology, morphology, syntax' tripod, it is not infrequently the weakest leg. Recent publications seem to indicate that the most fashionable technique is to eliminate syntax as a separate section since the components of the syntactic unit (phones in the shape of morphs) have already been totally inventoried in the two previous sections.

In the two leading overall descriptions of French, Maurice Grevisse, *Le bon usage* and Robert A. Hall, Jr., *Structural sketches / 1: French*,[1] the syntactic presentation is minimal (Hall) or scattered (Grevisse). A careful reader could emerge from these two studies without any concept that French syntax is an entity and that it embraces any other consideration than word order in a very general sense.

There are two works devoted exclusively to syntactic analysis: Andreas Blinkenberg, *L'ordre des mots en français moderne* and J. B. Ratermanis, *Eléments de syntaxe*.[2] The title of the former indicates its scope and approach, but its contents are definitive, once that limited methodology has been accepted. Blinkenberg deals solely with word order and treats continuous and discontinuous morphemes, inversions of subject and verb, dual representation of subject (usually as noun and pronoun). Ratermanis' highly organized work is an inventory of lexical items, grouped according to the word arrangement they condition. In a sense, his is a cause-and-effect methodology, assuming a lineal sequence of morphemes, each of which is partially conditioned by what precedes, and each of which likewise conditions that which follows. Blinkenberg has produced another study, *Le problème de l'accord en français moderne*[3] but, like the study of word order, it is concerned with one facet of syntax and is not a comprehensive total syntactic description.

An examination of these titles and works leads to the conclusion that the total composition of French syntax has many such facets: agreement, word order, lexical conditioning. No one facet, however, completely portrays French syntax, and the technique used for each facet will certainly not result in an exclusive methodology, if only because of the treatment of the other facets, the methodological identities of which should not be violated by a unilateral analysis. This compositeness may have eluded the linguist and fragmented any total view of French syntax.

These five studies show the results of various methodologies; but it is uncertain whether any one of the linguists involved had a concept of method applicable to syntax in its entirety. At this point, it would seem wise to examine in more detail (apart from the positive, concrete results and contributions of their work, the possibilities that their approaches present.

There are advantages in the conscientious application of at least three methodological techniques: the classification of syntactic units by parts of speech, the identification of cluster heads, and the positing of hypothetical structures in diagrammed shapes of arrangements.

To obtain a smaller and more workable segment of language, the word and thence the PART OF SPEECH is the logical and most facile point of departure, for it is the definition of a given part of speech that is, from many points of view, most clear syntactically. For example, a noun may occur exclusively as the only lexical entity immediately after a qualifier. Every French noun is operative in that syntactic environment, and all other parts of speech are not. While this may explain the noun, what does this particular methodological approach accomplish in terms of syntactic arrangement? It contributes the concept of 'slot' and 'filler' and a gross frame which may be enlightening in simple analyses and contrast. That there is a frame is undeniable. This technique further expedites the manipulation of the lexicon and the compilation of valuable lists, since the classification into words has already been accomplished (or assumed), and the linguist has immediate access to dictionary listings. But unfortunately, a description merely involved with gross and expeditious classes is no longer helpful; the 'misty flats' cohabited by noun and verb, for example, are in need of more illumination, and a parts-of-speech discussion of syntax is, as a last analysis, too elementary to be satisfying.

Where there are a few overt morphological markers, CLASSIFICATION of word clusters on the basis OF PHRASE HEAD has also been useful as a syntactic technique. As a methodology for defining gross categories, the application of this analytical apparatus to French is functional; however, it is even more revealing in its limitations. The phrase head in *près du chateau* is *chateau*, but the head of *donne-t-il* is more difficult to ascertain, although bound forms are not an exclusively French preoccupation. The difference between morphological head and syntactic head is difficult to see with precision.

Consider two clusters such as

> *parce qu'il m'a envoyé la lettre*
> *bien qu'il m'ait envoyé la lettre.*

Any classification, once progress has been made beyond parts of speech and lineal word order, is complicated by the obvious rapport between link and verb. (Questioning whether such rapport is in any way syntactic only reveals an inclination to think of syntax as a building-block assembly.) Classification into clusters and identification of cluster heads do not help in this intracluster rapport that is so commonly found in French.

Examination of hypothetical structures in DIAGRAMMED SHAPES OF ARRANGEMENT reveals a clear and objective view of lineal word order. It is possible to account for all utterance positions, all arrangements of which follow if a given position is occupied by a certain class member. However, we are again left with slots, fillers, and building blocks, which remain as gross but unrefined tools, like parts of speech. The interlacings, which are wholly environmental and therefore syntactic, are not accounted for, a grievous omission. In the morpheme inventory, there is the distinction made between continuous and discontinuous morphs; but if syntax is a series of lineal diagrams, eventually the problem of cataloging complete environmental conditioning is left unsolved. For example, the problem of sequence of tenses has been a linguistic pariah for French analysts; it belongs to no formal section of analysis, and is a stepchild of morphology and syntax. Since it involves morphological forms, adequately inventoried in the index of morphemes, there would seem to be no need to duplicate such a formal listing under another heading. But, in an utterance such as *Quand je le verrai, je le lui donnerai*, the morphological shape of the finite verb *donnerai* is due in some measure to its environment, that is, its position after the initial link *quand*, followed by a finite verb in future tense shape. Or another example: *Si je le vois, je le lui donnerai*. The verb shapes of both *vois* and *donnerai* are partly environmental and, hence, in analysis are syntactic. A diagram does not convey this rapport adequately, and therefore, diagramming is an incomplete methodology for French syntax.

For a description of French syntax, a study of the work of Blinkenberg, Grevisse, Hall, and Ratermanis reveals that all the following features are to be accounted for: (1) lineal word order, (2) discontinuous morpheme arrangement, (3) all morphemic environmental conditionings. A discussion of lineal word order must include an inventory of all potential orderings and lexical determinations of order. Discontinuous morpheme arrangement is concerned with the alternations in lineal word order because of the presence of discontinuous morphs of various classes. The principles or rules operative under all three sections of syntax are potentially co-occurrent.

A review of other syntactic methodologies shows that mere analysis by parts of speech, cluster heads, OR diagrams, while helpful initially, is not sufficient and does not produce sufficiently refined descriptions. The purpose of this paper is to discuss French verbal syntax as a tentative model, demonstrating the wholeness of syntax as a unit and the value of a variety of methodological approaches in combination.

The minimal unit of French verbs is defined in terms of the three features of syntax (lineal word order, discontinuous morpheme arrangement, and environmental conditionings)—a sequence of morphs containing all secondary or tertiary units of discontinuous morphemes and all resultant environmental conditionings. By this definition *Je ne l'ai pas ouverte* is one minimal syntactic unit, as contrasted with a breakdown like *Je ne l'ai pas | ouverte*. In all examples, environmental conditioning is maximal to facilitate exposition.

This minimal unit of French verbal syntax coincides with the so-called breath group. It is a phonetic, semantic, and morphological unit, definable in terms of pause, meaning conveyed, and the grammatical rules governing interior and exterior composition. Phonologically a breath group is a cluster of syllables between pauses. Since there is no so-called plus juncture in French, the single term 'pause' is functional and meaningful. Morphologically the breath group consists of a finite verb preceded and/or followed by subject pronoun, object pronoun(s), negative, past participle. In a description of the syntax of the French verbal breath group, it is necessary first to account for the internal order; 'internal' refers to order contained within breath-group boundaries, which may or may not have any connection with linguistic units occurring in other groups. Morphological or syntactic connections between different breath groups are 'external'.

The ordering of items within the minimal verb unit is fixed, predictable, and readily describable as a lineal sequence that is examinable (because of cultural and orthographic prejudice) from left to right. Items (1) through (4) below are representative French utterances, followed by a diagrammatic master shape of this ordering which identifies the occupants of all potential positions.

(1) *Vous ne les avez pas ouvertes.*
(2) *Ne les ouvrez pas.*
(3) *Ouvrez-les.*
(4) *Ne les avez-vous pas ouvertes?*

(5)

I	II	III	IV	V	VI	VII
Subject Pronoun	Negative	Object Pronoun	Finite Verb	Subject Object Pronoun	Negative	Past Participle

There are seven potential positions or slots for specific morphological shapes in the minimal syntactic unit, with certain observable features of ordering.

Position I is occupied by subject pronouns, one of a set of substantive class members showing accord with the units of position IV, the finite verb; these subject pronouns are not obligatory (2), may occur in position V instead of position I (4), and may be replaced in position I by a substantive which also shows accord with the units of position IV.

Positions II and VI in this minimal unit are always filled by the discontinuous negative morpheme, which is optional, and, for example, could be omitted from utterances (1) and (4) without altering the shape.

Position III is occupied by object pronouns, another set of substantive class members, of the same general type as those occupying position I. There is also fixed ordering of object pronouns. Subject and object pronouns may occur in position V (4), but they are always in complementary distribution.

The finite verb form in position IV is the sole required item of the series, and a minimal syntactic unit can consist of this one element. In three specific shapes it can stand as a free form (so-called 2nd person singular and 1st and 2nd persons plural), but in all other shapes, it is bound to the subject pronoun occurring in position I or V.

As stated above, position V may be occupied by subject or object pronouns in complementary distribution; if positions II and VI are filled (presence of the discontinuous negative morphemes), position V cannot be occupied by an object pronoun.

The occupant of position VII, the past participle, is a bound form, with the subject pronoun of position I or V.

This minimal syntactic unit is strengthened internally by fixed patterns of accord existing potentially between positions I and IV, I and VII, IV and V, V and VII, or III and VII. The accord between positions I and IV is always overt.

A listing of all the possible inner arrangements clearly shows that the key position for classification is position V.

(6) *Ouvrez-les.   Ne les ouvrez pas.*

Ouvrez-vous?   N'ouvrez-vous pas.
Avez-vous ouvert?   N'avez-vous pas ouvert.
Les ouvrez-vous?   Ne les ouvrez-vous pas.
Les avez-vous ouvertes?   Ne les avez-vous ouvertes.

Vous ouvrez.   Vous n'ouvrez pas.
Vous avez ouvert.   Vous n'avez pas ouvert.
Vous les ouvrez.   Vous ne les ouvrez pas.
Vous les avez ouvertes.   Vous ne les avez pas ouvertes.

Ouvrez.

By using the same position numbers as in example (5) above, and by listing these syntactic groups as numerical sequences, two patterns emerge: first, position v is occupied, either by subject or object pronouns; second, position I and v are both empty, or position one is filled, with position v still empty.

(7) A. IV – V   II – III – IV – VI

     B. IV – V   II – IV – V – VI
        IV – V – VII   II – IV – V – VI – VII
        III – IV – V   II – III – IV – V – VI
        III – IV – V – VII   II – III – IV – V – VI – VII

     C. I – IV   I – II – IV – VI
        I – IV – VII   I – II – IV – VI – VII
        I – III – IV   I – II – III – IV – VI
        I – III – IV – VII   I – II – III – IV – VI – VII

     D. IV

In class A in (7), there are only two variants, and the second is completely different from the first; in this class, position v is filled by an object pronoun. In class B in (7), position v is occupied by a subject pronoun; the position is full for each variant, and the internal ordering is relatively stable from variant to variant. The shape of the item occupying position v of class B is identical to the one filling position I of class C in (7). In fact, class B and class C are identical, if the filler of position v shifts to position I, or vice versa. Class C can be eliminated if it is called a potential derivation of class B, by changing position v to position I.

These numerical sequences also reveal strong syntactic bonds; with the assumption that some sort of syntactic bond exists between any two contiguous items, there is a striking frequency of occurrence of the III – IV – V pattern, or III – IV, or IV – V. In the minimal unit of French verbal syntax, these sequences would seem to be the strongest sets.

These numerical combinations represent a complete set of potential lineal arrangements within the minimal syntactic unit of French verbs. Any one of the sequences can be the code to a possible arrangement, and if the morphemic items are present, they will be present in that syntactic arrangement. In numerical terms, the minimal unit of verb syntax is any series of selected morphs (presumably inventoried under morphemes) bounded by any two fillers, I – IV on the left and IV – VII on the right. If there is only one morph, it must be IV, and this is the only possibility involving less than two morphs.

All three features of syntax thus far discussed (lineal word order, discontinuous morpheme arrangement, and environmental conditioning of lineal order) can be summarized in the diagram (8).

(8) Diagram of minimal syntactic unit of French verbal syntax

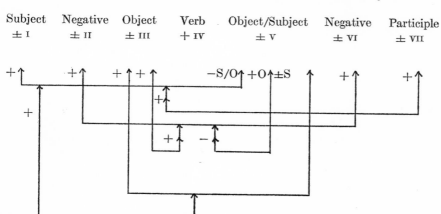

Subject	Negative	Object	Verb	Object/Subject	Negative	Participle
± I	± II	± III	+ IV	± V	± VI	± VII

+ —————— − = if one, not another; may be reversed

+ —————— + = if one, then another

In addition to its occurrence as the sole verbal unit, the minimal unit of verb syntax can occur as the first element in a series of verbal chains; once again the actual word sequence is fixed, and is lexically determined by the finite verb or participle present. There are three possible patterns:

(9)   A. *Faites voir.*   *Ne faites pas voir.*

      B. *Je veux le faire.*   *Je veux ne pas le faire.*
         Je veux y entrer.   *Je veux ne pas y entrer.*

      C. *Je tiens à partir.*   *Je tiens à ne pas partir.*
         Je tiens à le faire.   *Je tiens à ne pas le faire.*
         Je tiens à y entrer.   *Je tiens à ne pas y entrer.*

Using the same system of numerical positions, a master shape can be constructed with subsequent positional possibilities:

(10)

	I	II	III	IV	V
	Minimal Unit	Link	Negative	Object Pronoun	Nonfinite Verb
A.	I – V			I – V	
B.	I – IV – V			I – II – IV – V	
C.	I – II – V			I – II – III – V	
	I – II – IV – V			I – II – III – IV – V	

Pattern A in (10) is possible only after a half-dozen lexical items which happen to fulfill morphological functions in other environments, thus giving them the appearance of a subclass of French modals. In pattern B in (10), the object pronoun is optional, and may occur in another shape because of the following nonfinite verb. For pattern C in (10) the same is true, but the link is mandatory, and its close syntactic relation or bond to the preceding finite verb is clear because of the lack of change in its morphophonemic shape when contiguous to pronoun objects. (The link generally undergoes mandatory shape changes when contiguous with such shapes in other environments.) Statistically, verbs following pattern A are least frequent (6–12 members); pattern B is only slightly more productive (25 members); and pattern C is relatively widespread by comparison (150 members). In all chains the negative is a continuous element, and in no way alters the shape of the following object pronouns. The nonfinite verb of a chain may itself, with its preceding accoutrements of negative and/or object pronouns, function as a minimal unit and therefore as the first unit of a chain of type A, B, or C in (10). In a prolonged utterance, there is a potential gap between position I and positions II to V, where any number of breath groups conceivably may occur. Yet the close rapport between positions I and II, in spite of intervening material, is shown by the shape of the item in position II, which is invariable and lexically determined by the identity of the finite verb or participle occupying position I.

After an identification of the minimal verb unit, an account of lineal word order within the minimal verb unit, and an examination of the functioning of that minimal verb unit in expanded syntactic environments, there remain only patterns of accord for analysis (or sequence of tenses).

There are four patterns of tense sequence which can be classified according to the links used:

(11)   A. *Quand*: all tenses identical

      B. *Bien que* + subjunctive 1 | present or future
                     subjunctive 2 | other tense forms

      C. *Si* + present | future
            imperfect | conditional

      D. All others

The link and its minimal unit, the tense form of which is indicated in (11), may be the first syntactic element or may occur later; its position makes no difference in the tense shape of either verb.

There are 12 links calling for the conditions of *quand* and over 60 like *bien que*. A complete listing can be found in Grevisse. Only *au cas où* commands the sequence of tenses of *si*.

While this model is yet imperfect and uses a combination of methodological techniques (diagrams, lexical listing, general commentary), it seems to account for the features peculiar to the whole of French syntax through: (1) definition of syntactic units, (2) lineal order within syntactic units, (3) functioning between syntactic units, and (4) environmental conditioning or patterns of accord.

NOTES

1 Grevisse, 8th rev. ed. (Gemblaux, 1964); Hall, *Language* Suppl. 24:3 (1948).
2 Blinkenberg (Copenhagen, 1928–33); Ratermanis (Iowa City, 1963).
3 Blinkenberg (Copenhagen, 1950).

12

LOANWORDS IN LINGUISTIC DESCRIPTION:
A CASE STUDY FROM TANZANIA, EAST AFRICA

W. H. Whiteley

Certain lexical items in a given language may be classed as 'borrowed' rather than as 'native'. This fact is relatively unimportant or even impossible to determine, if a linguist is concerned solely with making a descriptive statement of a body of material culled at a particular time. Distinguished neither by their phonology nor by their morphology from the stock of native items, such borrowings or loans may be regarded as the legitimate interest of historical or sociological linguists rather than of those concerned with descriptive problems. Yet the descriptive linguist must recognize the legitimacy of the problem, if the incorporation of loans into the descriptive statement may be achieved most efficiently and effectively by recognizing coexistent systems at different levels, rather than by forcing everything into a single system. Africa offers a fertile field for studying loans: the language contacts, especially between African and non-African languages, vary enormously, in duration, quality, and intensity; and because the situation can be studied as a process, delicately related to a changing socio-cultural background, it offers a complex but fascinating—if somewhat neglected— area for research.[1]

In the present paper I wish to consider the structure and status of English loanwords among Swahili speakers in Dar-es-Salaam. Since the situation for Swahili is inadequately documented, a major objective of the paper is to establish patterns of assimilation at a phonological and morphological level, and to consider whether separate subsystems should be set up.[2] This, however, also requires a consideration of the distribution of loans in the speech of monolingual and bilingual speakers.[3] While there appears to be less variation in the incidence of loans in the speech of monolinguals, the incidence or nonincidence of loans varies significantly with context among bilingual speakers. A second objective of the paper, therefore, is to assess the possibility of correlating social contexts with styles of speech in such a way that a series of conversion rules[4] might be drawn up for each style once a description of standard Swahili phonology has been stated.

Material for this study derives from personal observations in Dar-es-Salaam over a number of years since 1949, especially during 1962–3 and from 1964 to date, supplemented by the published reports of the parliamentary debates (Hansard) in the National Assembly,[5] by perusal of the daily newspapers *Mwafrika* and *Ngurumo* for 1964, and by listening to the radio.

A brief account of the language situation in the capital is essential. Dar-es-Salaam has an African population approaching 125,000. About one-third of the people speak Zaramo—a local Bantu language, closely related to Swahili—as their first language, and about another third speak Bantu languages from areas within 150 miles of the city. Swahili is the national language of the United Republic of Tanzania:[6] it is taught in the educational system as a medium of instruction for the first six—soon to be seven—years of schooling,[7] and as a subject up to the Cambridge School Certificate level (after twelve years of education). It has figured in the syllabus of the University College at Dar-es-Salaam since 1964. It is commonly the language of communication between European and African, Asian and African, and between Africans whose first languages are different, and special attenuated forms of the language are characteristic between the two first-mentioned groups. For how many people Swahili is a first language is not known; nor, in bilingual homes, are the occasions known when Swahili is used, though there seems to be general agreement that Swahili is associated with the informal, relaxed, leisured, and popular aspects of life, while English is reserved for the formal, serious, official, and 'cultured' situations. There are also homes where English, Swahili, or local languages are all spoken as a matter of principle. Finally, Swahili is the language of city council meetings and of a majority of speakers in the National Assembly; it is the language of primary and district courts, the political party, and the trade unions, and of the national radio program.

English is taught as a required subject beginning with the third year in the majority of schools, and is the medium of instruction and taught as a subject from the sixth school year through the university level. Because it is an international language it commands resources for the continued refinement of teaching methods to which Swahili has never had access. In Africa, it has been the language of prestige for a number of years, and is regarded as a sine qua non for every educated citizen. It is effectively the language of the Civil Service, the high court, and the cinema. Under the present educational system any child who completes his primary education can hope to be functionally literate in both English and Swahili, but hitherto the material rewards of life encouraged all who could to expend extra efforts on further acquisition of English, in however half-hearted and unsystematic a way.

The situation is thus one in which the two languages coexist: educational and cultural aspirations contributing to the wider use of English; national pride and prestige to the wider use of Swahili.[8]

Two general observations about the comparative structure of words in the two languages should precede a discussion of the details of phonological assimilation. Firstly, all Swahili words[9] have a final vowel so that, in establishing rules from a comparison of nonfinal English vowels with their realizations in Swahili, the question of the shape of the final vowel will usually require a different basis for prediction. Secondly, word stress is usually penultimate in Swahili.

Basically, loans are either phonologically assimilated or they are not, but within this dichotomy a number of subdivisions must be recognized. Firstly, at a given moment in time assimilated loans may be what I term 'established' or 'probationary'. Established loans are those that have been in 'general'[10] use for a number of years. Some go back to the 1920's,[11] while others already have secondary or tertiary connotations—usually of a probationary nature.[12] Established loans may be exemplified by such words as *baisikéli* 'bicycle';[13] *motokáa* 'motor vehicle'; *Desémba* 'December'; *rédio* 'radio'; *shílingi, shilíngi* 'shilling'; *kádi* 'card' (general). Probationary loans are those that, for one reason or another, are not yet in general use. These include colloquial and slang words and phrases, as well as a large number of words for which nonacceptance is most closely associated with their unfamiliarity, e.g.: *paréto* 'pyrethrum'; *sateláiti* 'satellite'; *bóni* 'a native of Dar-es-Salaam'; *kipléfiti* 'a traffic island'; *lófa* 'pauper, beggar'; *sánsuti* 'sunsuit'.

Each of these categories may again be divided into 'conformist' and 'innovatory' assimilations. Within these two groups, conformist words represent a substantial majority and merely constitute assimilations to the existing patterns of Swahili, e.g.: *shilíngi, deréva* 5/6 'driver', *lívu* 'leave' (police, army, and holidays and vacations generally). The latter introduce an innovation, such as a shift in the stress pattern (e.g. *sánsuti; kámpuni*), or a consonant cluster (e.g. *skrúbu* 'screw'; *mtápta* 'interpreter').

Unassimilated loans, which may be either single words or phrases, may also be divided: those in which there is no assimilation at any level, and those in which some assimilation—usually morphological—occurs. The former occur commonly in the speech of bilinguals and, in contrast with the findings of Uriel Weinreich,[14] it is not uncommon for whole phrases to occur within a single sentence, e.g. *nilikuwa nikimwambia* 'that fellow when who arrived', but *rafiki yangu John P. from Tanga nikamwambia ...* 'I was telling that fellow when who arrived but my friend John P. from Tanga, and I told him ...' Established and probationary forms may possibly have to be recognized, but as an unassimilated loan becomes established it will also probably become assimilated. Partially unassimilated loans are extremely common among bilinguals and usually comprise an unassimilated root or stem, with an appropriate Swahili affix, e.g. *ma-girls* heard as [magəːlz], similarly *u-pilot* [upáilɔt], *nime-advise* [nimeədvaiz],[15] and *ina-convey nini maneno haya mawali* [kɔnvéi] 'What do these two words connote?' Committee meetings are rich sources for such loans![16] The above divisions may be represented schematically as in the diagram below.

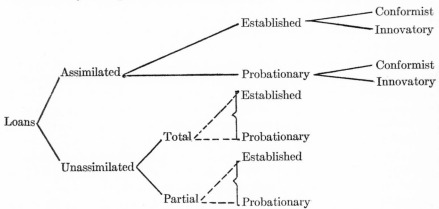

The occurrence or nonoccurrence of loans in any given situation is dictated largely by one or more of three major factors: (1) the subject of discourse, (2) the nature of the social context, and (3) the education and outlook of the speaker. The qualification is important, however, because of the number of independent variables. The factors themselves are by no means clearly defined nor exclusive, but serve rather as areas around which some generalization may occur. This, of course, is also true of the various divisions of loans that I have suggested above. They, too, are arbitrary and the contents are likely to be disputed by different speakers.

(1) The first of the three factors concerns the subject of discourse. In discussing technical and semitechnical terms, loans inevitably occur, but their status as established, probationary, or unassimilated loans depends partly on the nature of the subject and partly on the speaker. For example, a technical subject such as the 'automobile' provides an interesting example of the range of possible solutions. First there are technical words for which no equivalents as yet exist. They may be retained unassimilated, e.g.: *dynamo* [dáinəmo], *kingpin* [kíŋpɪn], *tie-rod end* [táirədend], *points* [póints], *rotor-arm* [routə]; or they may be assimilated, e.g.: *shoka(o)mzoba* 'shock absorber', *difréncha* 'differential', *ékseleta* 'accelerator', *sp(i)ríngi* 'spring', *bólti* 'bolt', *kláchi* 'clutch'. Second are the technical words for which terms have been invented, these being for the most part nonloans with other connotations, e.g.: *kichujio cha mafuta* 'oil filter', *kibuyu* 'air cleaner', *usukani* 'steering wheel' (also [sté:liŋ]), *mkanda* 'fan belt' (also [fánbelt]), *shoo ya gari* 'radiator grill', *ngao ya mbele/nyuma* 'rear/front bumper', *máflo* 'silencer' (der. muffler). Third are the nontechnical words for which

terms already exist and whose meanings may be extended, e.g.: *kipaa* 'roof', *kioo* 'mirror', *mlango* 'door', *kiti* 'seat', *kifungulio cha dirisha* 'window-winder'. Furthermore, some speakers will avoid using a loan on principle—using *mpira* rather than *táili* 'tire', *mtambo* rather than *swíchi* 'switch', *manjanika* rather than *wínchi*, *kizuio* rather than *insuléta* 'insulator', and *kisawazisha joto* rather than *thé:mostat*. With the passage of time some of these doublets will doubtless acquire specialized connotations, as has *rezolushéni* for 'technical resolutions' as opposed to the more general *azimio*.

By contrast, there are some subjects that do not appear to attract loans: while many basic terms for articles of clothing are established loans, terms for fashions in clothes, hairstyles, jewelry, etc. seem less often to be loans than loan translations or descriptive terms from Swahili.[17] Sport, however, especially football, is associated with an extensive use of both established and probationary loans, and provides a rich source for extended connotations.[18] The army and police are also important sources.

Finally, there are some subjects of discourse that are themselves conditioned by more or less deliberate policy. In the field of legal terminology a conscious effort is being made to provide Swahili equivalents; there is heavy dependence on Arabic loans, but virtually no borrowing from English. On the other hand, in the field of medicine the general policy is to use unassimilated English terms.

(2) Some social contexts appear to impose their own patterns on discourse. There are firstly the informal situations, such as the dance hall, bar, tearoom, street corner, and market, where the participants are usually young and sometimes delinquent. Probationary loans are extremely common in their conversations, which are also characterized by nonce words and neologisms from Swahili and other Bantu languages. Such colloquialisms and slang words are referred to as *kihuni* 'slang, street talk' by the older, more respectable members of society.[19] There are also more formal situations, including council and committee meetings and serious discussions of various kinds in which the participants may be older, more sophisticated bilinguals. Here, partially and totally assimilated loans are extremely common, and a man who would not be heard using a colloquialism like *lófa* 'pauper' has no hesitation in saying *maana ameki-meditate* [mɛditɛit] 'because he has thought about it'. Furthermore, such bilinguals possess the highest degree of language flexibility; such speakers may move freely from assimilation to unassimilation, using 'Regional Commissioner' in one sentence and *Rejenokamíshna* in the next.

An interesting sidelight on the use of loans in a given social situation is provided by debates in the National Assembly. A sample of 25,000 words from a recent Hansard showed an overall incidence of 1 percent of established loans, though this rose to around 10 percent during the discussion of such technicalities as wireless licenses. The overall occurrence of totally unassimilated loans was somewhat under 1 percent, while that of partially assimilated loans was confined to a mere handful. All loans in the sample, with only two exceptions, were nouns.

(3) People's educational level may be viewed in terms of a single scale. Toward one end are monolinguals, who on the whole form an older segment of the population, and who tend to use only established loans. Toward the other end are the highly educated bilinguals, who tend to comprise the younger generation of the population and who are particularly addicted to the use of totally or partially unassimilated loans. At all points along the scale are individuals who, for one reason or another, take a sharply positive or negative attitude toward the use of loans.

The foregoing may be summarized as follows: use of established or probationary loans is the important factor in instances where the subject of conversation or discussion is technical or semitechnical. Certain informal social contexts, however, impose a pattern of probationary loans, plus nonce words and neologisms from Swahili and other Bantu languages. Finally, a high degree of education seems itself to impose a pattern on the occurrence of loans, in this case of totally or partially unassimilated loans. In extreme cases there appears to be no point in talking about loans at all, since the speaker is really using two languages simultaneously. It would be difficult to assign priorities to the three factors, but I believe education to be the most important, then the subject of discourse, and finally the social context.

Because there is a very close connection between the spoken and written word, the occurrence of loans in the press merits some discussion. In a daily paper like *Ngurumo*, established loans may occur in any article. The fact that they are less frequent in the correspondence columns may be indicative of the importance of the 'written' context for a speaker. Probationary loans are especially common in reports of court cases and in gossip columns. Of these probationary loans, orthographic representations may attempt to reproduce three things: (1) the sound of the word, e.g. *afrikanaizesheni*, *kuripoti* 'to report'; (2) the shape of the word, e.g. *-piga starti*; (3) or both, e.g. *kurekordi* 'to make a recording', *korti* 'court', which are realized in speech as [kurɛkɔdi] and [kɔ́:ti], cf. *kóti* 'coat'. Attempts to retain the English spelling in the loan may lead the unfamiliar reader to treat the representation as though it were Swahili, which in turn would lead to the use of the 'one-tap *r*' and an additional vowel, as in [kurɛkɔrdi] or [kurɛkɔridi]. By contrast, the English noun 'lease' has, for some reason, been assimilated as *lizi*[20] and this has led to its realization in the English of bilinguals as [li:z] on the assumption that if it is a loanword from English this must be its English realization.

Table 1 represents my synopsis of the sound systems of Standard Swahili and English. Such a presentation is convenient, but it is also misleading since there is no way of knowing from what system or subsystem any given loan is actually taken. Furthermore, it is not easy to decide whether a given sound should be stated as similar or dissimilar to one cited for another language. For example, at least one common variant of the English *r*— the frictionless continuant—is quite unknown in Swahili. Should the English *r* be marked as nonoccurring? Similarly, the short open back vowel ɒ is close to, but more open than the Swahili *o*. If facts such as these are taken into account, the table can still serve a useful purpose.

TABLE 1. SYNOPSIS OF THE SOUND SYSTEMS OF STANDARD SWAHILI AND ENGLISH

   Voiced stops may be imploded for speakers of coastal origin; in unvoiced stops aspiration may be distinctive. Vowel length is not significant; word stress is usually penultimate; word tone is not significant.
   Items enclosed within brackets do not occur in the other language. Items enclosed within parentheses for Swahili represent phonetic transcriptions.

Swahili (standard orthography)*	English†
p, t, k, b, d, [j (ɟ)], g	p, t, k, b, d, g
m, n, ny, ng' (ŋ)	m, n, ŋ
ch (tʃ)	tʃ, [dʒ]
f, v, s, z, th (θ), dh (ð), gh (γ), h	f, v, s, z, θ, ð, ʃ, [ʒ], h
l, r	l, r
w, y	w, y
Clusters (nasal only)	Clusters
Initial/medial: mb, nd, ng, nj, nk, nz	Initial/medial: br, dr, kr, fr, pr, tr, spr, str, skw, skr, gr, thr, kw, gw, tw
	Medial/final: mp, mb, nt, nd, ŋg, ŋk, tl, tn, mf, mth, ns, nth, nz, prl
	Both: bl, kl, fl, pl, tl, sp, etc.
i, e, a, o, u	[ɪ], e, [æ], ɒ, [ʊ, ʌ, ə], i:, [ɑ:], ɔ:, u:, [ɜ:], [eɪ, aɪ, ɔɪ, əʊ(oʊ), aʊ], [ɪə, ɛə, ʊə]

   * The most detailed study to date is that by A. N. Tucker and E. O. Ashton, 'Swahili phonetics', *African studies* 1:2–3.77–103, 161–82 (1942) for the dialect in the town of Zanzibar.
   † The transcription adopted here is that of A. C. Gimson, *An introduction to the pronunciation of English* (London, 1962). I have also consulted Daniel Jones, *The pronunciation of English* (Cambridge, Eng., 1950).

DETAILED EXAMINATION OF ASSIMILATED LOANS

I do not attempt in the following list of loans to distinguish between established and probationary loans which, as noted above, may vary from speaker to speaker.

In Bantu linguistics it is customary to classify nouns[21] according to the shape of prefixes associated with them, and these are usually numbered thus: 1/2 *m-/wa-* ; 3/4 *m-/mi-* ; 5/6 *ji-/ma-* or zero/*ma+* ; 7/8 *ki-/vi-* ; 9/10 *n-/n-* or zero/zero, up to 19. The slash (/) stands for 'and'; the numerals refer to particular forms of a prefix, e.g. 5/6 means 'occurs with prefixes 5 and 6.' Except where noted, nouns belong to noun classes 9/10. Verbs are cited in their root form preceded by a hyphen.

VOWELS

V1. Eng. *i:, ɪ* → Sw. *i*

An open variant analogous to the English short vowel has been increasingly noted medially and in unstressed positions.[22]

vayalíni 'violin'	*gíta, gitáa* 'guitar'
pákiti, pákti 'packet'	*siménti* 'cement'
zípu 'zip-fastener'	*díshi* 'dish' (of various kinds)
sinéma 'cinema'	*filímu* 'film' (of camera)
mashíne, mashíni 'machine'	*spídi* 'speed'
-rikódi 'record'	*pícha* 'picture, photograph'
nótisi 'notice'	*afísi* 'office' (see V4 below)
afísa 'officer' (see V4 below)	*polísi* 'police', e.g. *mtu wa polisi*
kabíchi 'cabbage'	*téksi, tékisi* 'taxi'
kámpuni, kampúni 5/6 'company'	*ripóti* 'report'
wíki 'week'	*tímu* 'team'
lívu 'leave' (police, army)	*stímu* 'electricity'
lízi 'lease'	*-ripéa* 'repair'

There are a number of exceptions. Of these, *géa* 'gear', *biskúti* 'biscuit', and *róketi* 5/6, 9/10 'rocket' appear to have been assimilated on the basis of their English spelling. The form *kamáti* 'committee' I believe to have been the personal creation of the late Shaaban Robert, who disliked *kamiti* which was current about 1956–7. For the last two examples I have no explanation: *rumánde, lumánde* 'remand' and *bigáme* 'bigamy'.

V2. Eng. *e* → Sw. *e*

jéti 'jet aircraft'	*-béti* 'gamble, bet'
siménti 'cement'	*hotéli* 'hotel'
sinéma 'cinema'	*déski* 'desk'
televishéni 'television'	*chéki* 'check'
mémba 'member'	*gazéti* 'newspaper'
péni '10-cent piece', cf. *pé:ni* 'pen'	*kipléfiti* 7/8 'traffic island'
vésti 'vest, singlet'	*penhóda* 'penholder'

The only exception I have recorded is *ínjini* 'engine', and it is possible that this was assimilated from the variant English form [ɪndʒɪn].

V3. Eng. æ → Sw. *a, e*

At the time of Tucker's[23] earlier work, *a* was the more common realization, and there is reason to believe that the present realization in *e* is of recent occurrence.

spána 'spanner'

kalénda, kálenda 'calendar'

bangíli 'bangle'

károti, karóti 'carrot'

gange 5/6 'job' (der. gang), cf.
  genge 5/6 'gang' (of thugs, etc.)

fulána 'vest, singlet'

jakéti 'jacket'

sténdi 'bus stand'

késhi 'cash'

géreji 'garage'

pákiti 'packet'

trákta, trakíta, trékta 5/6 'tractor'

stámpu, stémpu 'stamp' (postage)

bánki, bénki 'bank'

makánika 'mechanic'

bégi 'bag' (esp. briefcase)

méchi 'football match'

béndi 'band, orchestra'

jém(u) 'jam, preserve'

V4. Eng. ɒ, ɔ: → Sw. *o*

The realizations *ofísa* 'officer' and *ófisi, ofísi* 'office' are now not favored. See V4 exceptions: *afísa, afísi*.

lóri 5/6 'lorry'

sóksi 'socks'

poketimáni 5/6 'small change'
  (der. pocket money), cf.
  poketiméni 5/6 'pickpocket'
  (der. pocket man)

konsélu 'consul'

sipitáli, hospitáli 'hospital'

rokéti, róketi 5/6, 9/10 'rocket'

koléji 'college'

ukolóni 14 'colonialism'

For the few exceptions to this pattern I have no explanation (other than that of spelling assimilation as noted above):

afísa 'officer' (see V7)

kunduráti 'contract'

afísi 'office'

daktári 'doctor'

tóchi 'torch'

kórti 5/6, 9/10 'court'

ripóti 5/6, 9/10 'report'

fórmu, fómu 'form, grade in school'

dróo 'drawer' (of a cupboard)

bóni 5/6 'native of Dar-es-Salaam'
  (der. born)

stóo 'store'

hóli 'hall'

-rikódi 'record'

yunifómu 'uniform'

kóna 5/6 'corner'

For the single exception recorded to date I can offer no explanation: *cháki* 'chalk'.

V5. Eng. ʊ, *u:* → Sw. *u*

There are relatively few loans to be noted here:

fúti 'foot, foot rule'

skúta 'scooter'
skrúbu 'screw'
kupóni 'coupon'

muzíki, múziki 'music'
súti 'suit'
bulúu, blúu 'blue'
tyúbu 'tube'

V6. Eng. ʌ → Sw. *a*

bási 'bus'
pámpu 'pump' (esp. bicycle)
námba, nambári 'number'
kámpuni, kampúni 5/6 'company'
páncha 'puncture'
táni 'ton', cf. *tá:ni ya kulia*
 'right-turn', and *raitá:ni*
plági 'plug (spark-)'
rába 'rubber'

kabáti 'cupboard'
bráshi, buráshi 'brush'. The latter
 is the older assimilation.
kilábu 7/8 'club'
jáji 5/6 'judge'
lokápu 'a lockup, jail'
fanéli 'funnel' (medical)
ráfu adj. (invariable) 'rough' (esp.
 of sport)

Again, for the single exception I offer no explanation: *tarumbéta* 'trumpet'.

V7. Eng. ə, ɜː → Sw. *a*

alvánzi 'advance' (of money, pay-
 ment)
pátina 'partner'
sekondári 'secondary' (school)
léseni 'license'
mtápta 1/2 'interpreter'
deréva 5/6 'driver'
méya 'mayor'
kamáti 'committee'
bía 'beer'
vócha 'voucher'

adrési 'address'
pícha 'picture, photograph'
kamíshna 1/2, 5/6 'commissioner'
afísa, áfisa 'officer'
kóna 'corner'
éka 'acre'
skúta 'scooter'
wáya 'wire'
afrikanaizésheni 'Africanization'
póda 'powder' (face, talcum, etc.)
mashíne 'machine'

There are a number of exceptions. For most of these a subsidiary rule applies: if the schwa occurs in the penultimate stressed position in the loan, it will be assimilated as *e*:

beséni 'basin'
rezolushéni 'formal resolution'
konsélu 'consul'

leséni, léseni 'license'
televishéni 'television'

For two others the subsidiary rule applies that if the schwa follows a labial, it will be assimilated to *u*: *kampúni* 5/6 'company' and *tá(w)ulo* 'towel'. For still a few others no explanation can be offered:

táili 'tire'

károti 'carrot' (analogy with
written form?)

sháti 'shirt'
-*sáchi* 'search' (esp. of police)

mtápta 1/2 'interpreter'
fówad(i) 5/6 'forward' (football)

There is a single exception for which no explanation can be offered: *skíti* 'skirt'.

V8. Eng. ɑː → Sw. *a*

báa 'bar'
yádi 'yard'
sájini 'sergeant'
gitáa, gíta 'guitar'
dánsi 'dance'
skáfu 'head-scarf'
-*piga starti* [stɑːti] 'start a car'
motokáa 'motor vehicle'

pátina 'partner'
stáfu 5/6 'modern, educated person' (also the 'staff of an organization' [der. staff]. This is also the realization for the English 'stuff' [n] which sometimes occurs with the connotation of 'unwanted material, rubbish'.)

DIPHTHONGS

With the exception of *eı*, *oʊ/əʊ* diphthongs are assimilated as vowel sequences of the quality most closely related to the English qualities. There has been for some years now (Tucker, 1946) a marked tendency, not restricted to loans, to realize vowel sequences as glides. This tendency has been given a marked impetus with the spread of English.

D1. Eng. *aı* → Sw. *ai*

fáini 'fine'
tái 'tie'
táili 'tire'
táiti 'tight-fitting dress'
nailóni 'nylon'
laif(u) 'life'[24]

táifod 'typhoid fever'
páinti 'pint'
stáili 'style'
taipuráita 'typewriter'
naizésheni 5/6 'a *jumped-up* person'

There are one or two exceptions which require subsidiary rules: if the diphthong is followed by a vowel, the whole is assimilated as *ay* + vowel, e.g. *wáya* 'wire', and *sáyansi* 'science'. There are one or two other exceptions for which no explanation is offered at this stage: *léseni, leséni* 'license' and *deréva* 5/6 'driver', but the latter is a loan of long standing and would have to have been assimilated at a time when consonant clusters were still unacceptable.

D2. Eng. *eɪ* → Sw. *e*

kéki 'cake'	*bréki* 'brake'
kési 5/6, 9/10 'case' (court)	*éka* 'acre'
jéla 5/6 'jail'	*rédio* 'radio'
-féli 'fail' (esp. examination)	*epróni* 'apron' (in printing)
sepéto/-u 'spade'	*tébo* 'mathematical table'

For neither of the two exceptions recorded can an explanation be offered: *kábe* 'cable', *ajénti* 'agent'.

D3. Eng. *ɔɪ, ɪə, ɛa, ʊə, aʊ* → Sw. *oi, ia, ea, ua, au*

táifod 'typhoid fever'	*aría* 'area'
bía 'beer'	*skwéya* 'square'
-ripéa 'repair'	*skáuti* 5/6 'scout' (boy scout)
gáuni 'dress'	*páuni* 'pound'
blaúzi 'blouse' (also 7/8 *kikóti*)	*áunsi* 'ounce'

Of the exceptions, some exemplify the diphthong/vowel sequence noted above, e.g. *vayalíni* 'violin', *wáya* 'wire'; others, like *géa*, probably represent assimilation from the written form. A well-established alternative assimilation for Eng. *aʊ* occurs with Sw. *o*:

vócha 'voucher'	*póchi* 'pouch'
kóchi 'couch'	*póda* 'powder' (face, talcum, etc.)

D4. Eng. *oʊ/əʊ* → Sw. *o*

nóti 'note'	*kóti* 'coat'
notísi 'notice'	*pósta* 'post office'
lófa 5/6 'pauper, beggar'	*motabóti* 'motorboat'
háro 'harrow'	

The results of this detailed examination of vowel assimilation can be summarized in a series of predictive rules which operate for the majority of loans. Total ability to predict is unlikely; loans are introduced by people, and even through personal idiosyncrasy. Some eccentric forms are noted later.

Rules:		
(i)	Eng. iː, ɪ	→ Sw. i
(ii)	Eng. e, ɛɪ, æ, ə (penultimate stressed)	→ Sw. e
(iii)	Eng. ə, ɜː, ʌ, ɑː	→ Sw. a
(iv)	Eng. ɒ, ɔː, oʊ(əʊ)	→ Sw. o
(v)	Eng. ʊ, uː	→ Sw. u
(vi)	Eng. final labial: f, v, m, p, b	→ Sw. u (final)
(vii)	Eng. final postlabial	→ Sw. i (final) a, o, e rarely
(viii)	Eng. final 'dark' l	→ Sw. o (final)

Rule (vi), noted by Růžička (1953) and by earlier mission Bible translators, seems likely to apply with certain modifications to loans from Arabic, and possibly even to nonloans where the final vowel cannot definitely be established as a deverbative formation. Rule (viii) is attested from a fairly small sample, the *l* being replaced or followed by *o*, e.g. *tébo, kóplo, máflo*.

Diphthongs not included above are realized as vowel sequences, increasingly as vowel glides, in which the quality of the components is that closest to the English.

CONSONANTS

Consonants present few problems. In general, the English consonants are assimilated to the equivalent sound in Swahili; the voiced affricate *dʒ*, for example, being assimilated as the palatal stop *j*. While examples both of voicing and of devoicing occur, no regular pattern is apparent: *risávu* 'reserve', *alvánzi* 'advance' (financial), *lízi* 'lease'.

Consonant clusters, however, do not occur in Swahili and in the earlier period of borrowing an anaptyctic vowel was common. Recent loans, on the other hand, reflect an increasing tendency to assimilate clusters, especially in medial position:

skúta 'scooter'
skwéya 'square'
tarumbéta 'trumpet'
skrúbu 'screw'
flána, fulána 'vest, singlet'
trékta 'tractor'
alvánzi 'advance' (financial)
petróli 'petrol'
dróo 'drawer' (of a cupboard)
kamíshna 'commissioner'

míksi 'mixed train'
mófti adj. 'smart, clean'
taitfíti 'tight-fitting dress'
páncha 'puncture'
daktári 'doctor'
mtápta 'interpreter'
konstébo 'constable' (police)
epróni 'apron' (in printing)
sábseti 'subset'

While such clusters are undoubtedly on the increase, it is not yet clear which are likely to become established, and no general prediction seems possible at this date.

Before concluding this discussion on phonological assimilation, I should point out that there are some loans in which the shape represents one or more eccentric assimilations. Some of these represent individual innovation; some, assimilation by writing rather than by speech; others, assimilation to sounds or clusters that are unknown or difficult in the host language. The following provide examples:

mtápta 'interpreter'
kunduráti 'contract'
manispáa 'municipality'
léseni 'license'

kóplo 'corporal' (army, police)
pínz(i) 'pea(s)'. This is one of the very rare examples of a loan with a final consonant.

MORPHOLOGICAL ASSIMILATION

In general, words are assimilated as units, but there are some cases in which only part of a word is accepted as a loan. The best example of this at the present time is the word *naizésheni* 'a jumped-up person, one who has benefited from the effects of *afrikanaizésheni*' (*kajifanya naizésheni kumbe jizi* 'He made himself look like a *nouveau riche*, it turned out he was a real thief'). The interesting hybrid forms *ndugunaizésheni* and *shemejenaizésheni* for 'brotherization' and 'in-law-ization' are currently common. There are other loans in which part of the English stem is assimilated as a prefix; this situation occurs most commonly with the prefixes *ki-* and *ma-*:

digádi pl. *madigádi* 'mudguard'   *ching'óda* pl. *maching'óda* 'marching
kipléfiti 'traffic island'   order'

The noun-class affiliation of loans varies. Loans in which the initia^l elements resemble prefixes, as in the above examples, will tend to operate these prefixes. Other loans tend to operate either 9/10 or 5/6 prefixes. Members of both these classes are characterized commonly by an initial zero-prefix, and the decision of the speaker to allocate a given loan to one of these classes depends on various factors not always accessible. Size is certainly important: large things tend to be allocated to class 5/6 and small things to 7/8, e.g. *maLéndrova*, 'land-rovers' (vehicles), but *viji-Folksvagen* 'volkswagens'. Similarly, nouns denoting persons tend to operate verbal prefixes of 1/2.

While loan verbs tend to be characterized by a final *-i* in their simple form, e.g. *-feli* 'fail' (esp. examination), *-pasi* 'pass' (an examination, and generally), *-sachi* 'search', they nevertheless operate a full series of tense signs and extended forms.

As an illustration of the operation of loans in a written context I have selected a passage reporting a football match (the italics are mine):

Ndipo mpira, ukaanza *timu* zote mbili zilicheza nguvu moja hakuna aliyemwachia mwenziwe lakini *senta hafu* hodari wa Kenya Style aitwae Mfum, alizuwiya nyuma hata *mafowad* hawakuweza kupita kwa urahisi Mfum alitoa *pasi* nzuri kwa Majid *hafu beki left* nae *akampasia* Hemed na Hemed *akampasia* Kurunguja ndipo akatoa mkwaju ukamfika Housband na kupiga bila kungoja ikiwa moja kwa moja hadi ikawa Kenya Style ikapata *goli* moja. Ngoma ikawekwa kati ulipoanza mpira *senta hafu* wa Rufiji Salamba akatoa *pasi* kwa *insaid rait* Mikumo lakini *chenta hafu* Mfumo walichengana vizuri ikawa Mfumo kaushika ikapigwa *peneti eria* aliyepiga ni Mikomo ikawa *goli* moja kwa moja.[25]

The first point to notice is the relatively high incidence of loans—almost 15 percent. These, with the exception of the four words with final consonant, are all assimilated according to the above rules. The selection of personal prefixes is also noticeable (*mafowad* hawaku——), and an ex-

tremely interesting feature is the adoption of Swahili word order, noun +
adjective, in the case of *hafu beki left* and, later in the same account (but
unquoted), *wingi raiti*. Such inversion is also noticeable in the well-established *steshéni polísi* 'police station'. This is a feature common also in
popular song, e.g. *freni mai* 'my friend'.

In this paper it has been possible to establish rules for vowel and consonant assimilation in established loans, but not possible to make any
useful predictive statements about the assimilation of consonant clusters.
We can say, therefore, with some confidence what shape a loan will assume.
What we cannot say with such confidence is whether—if a speaker uses a
loan at all—he will use an assimilated or unassimilated, established or
probationary loan, even though some general guidelines have been suggested. These guidelines are most viable in the case of technical or semitechnical subjects of discourse, and most tentative over a wide range of
other contexts. Intensive studies of usage by bilinguals over a range of
social situations will undoubtedly make possible a general increase in
viability. In this multilingual urban context where linguistic loyalties are
liable to sudden and profound change, the role of the individual as innova-
tor must not be forgotten, in an area where even the limits of innovation
are as yet only imperfectly charted. Particular account should be taken of
overall changes in the fashion of language.[26] Until recently it was fashionable to use Arabic loans and sounds in some circles; since 1964–5, however,
there has been some attempt to introduce and popularize Bantu loans,
e.g. *ikulu*, for the State House (der. Gogo) and *bunge* for the National
Assembly (der. Ha), and to play down the use of Arabic loans. Who sets a
fashion is difficult to determine, but I suspect that the educated elite are
doing it for partially assimilated and unassimilated loans, and that the
artisans, who are perhaps minimally bilingual, are setting the fashion in
assimilated loans. Whether such a trend will continue depends on un-
predictable factors. Finally, after considering the occurrence of loans in
Dar-es-Salaam, it is reasonable to ask whether the mere use of loans in any
language constitutes a special style of discourse. I suggest that the answer
should be in the negative.

On the other hand, where additional features characterize the discourse,
it is legitimate to talk of special styles, and I have observed at least three
major styles. Firstly, where the speaker is in a special situation such as
that of radio announcer, there are intonational features that clearly represent interference from English, and an important subdivision of this style
is that associated with radio advertising. A second style occurs when the
speaker intersperses his discourse with English phrases, with concomitant
switches of intonation patterns. A third style is used by the less educated

of the younger generation and is characterized by probationary loans, nonce words, neologisms, rapid 'turn-over' of vocabulary, and certain idiosyncrasies of syntax. Consideration of these and other current styles remains as the objective of further study.

NOTES

1   The general situation is admirably summarized by J. H. Greenberg in his 'The study of language contact in Africa', *Symposium on multilingualism* held at Brazzaville in 1962, Conseil scientifique pour l'Afrique / Commission de cooperation technique en Afrique, Publication no. 87.167–75 (London, 1964).

    A full bibliography of material on loans in African languages is beyond the scope of the present paper, but it is worth noting two areas which have recently received attention. The emergence of an urban *lingua franca* on the Zambia Copperbelt is discussed in A. L. Epstein, 'Linguistic innovation and culture on the Copperbelt, Northern Rhodesia' *Southwestern journal of anthropology* 15.235–53 (1959) and followed up by I. Richardson 'Some observations on the status of Town Bemba in Northern Rhodesia', *African language studies* 2.25–36 (1961) and 'Examples of deviation and innovation in Bemba' *ALS* 4.128–45 (1963). The position of loanwords in Hausa is discussed by F. W. Parsons, 'English loan-words in Hausa' (paper read before the Philological Society of Great Britain, 1959) and 'Some observations on the contact between English and Hausa', *Symposium on multilingualism* 197–203 (1964). Note also his reference to C. A. Nuttall, *Phonological interference of Hausa with English; A study in English as a second language* (unpubl. MA thesis, Victoria Univ. of Manchester, Eng., 1961–2). Other references might include: D. P. Kunene, 'Southern Sotho words of English and Afrikaans origin', *Word* 19.347–75 (1963); A. Demoz, 'European loanwords in an Amharic daily newspaper', *Language in Africa*, John Spencer, ed. 116–22 (Cambridge, 1963); W. H. Whiteley, 'Loan-words in Kamba; A preliminary survey', *ALS* 4.146–65 (1963); and the *Symposium on multilingualism* (1964).

2   The most detailed loanword study to date for Swahili is K. M. Růžička's 'Lehnwörter im Swahili / I', *Archiv Orientalni* 21.582–603 (1953); in general his findings from written sources are corroborated by my own observations a decade later. Another detailed study, which I have not yet seen, is H. Höftmann's thesis, 'Untersuchung zur Eingliederung moderner Begriffe in Bantusprachen' *Ethnographisch-Archäologische Zeitschrift* 4.60–5 (1963). A more limited study, again based on written sources, is that by W. Bühlmann, 'Principles of phonetic adaptation in Swahili applied to Christian names', *Africa* 23.127–34 (1953). A. N. Tucker's 'Foreign sounds in Swahili', *Bulletin of the school of Oriental and African studies* 11:4.854–71 (1946); 12:1.214–32 (1947) is based mainly on the speech of a Zanzibari informant. Interesting but unsystematic observations occur in R. H. Gower's 'Swahili borrowings from English', *Africa* 22:2.154–7 (1952) and in his 'Swahili slang', *Journal of the East African Swahili Committee* 28:2.41–8 (1958); the latter is amplified by J.

A. K. Leslie, 'Swahili slang: Further notes', *JEASC* 29:1.81–4 (1959). In similar vein is F. A. Reynolds, 'Lavu huzungusha dunia', *Tanganyika notes and records* nos. 58–9.203–4 (1962).

3   These terms are used in a rather special sense: by monolingual I mean here a person who speaks Swahili but not English, irrespective of the number of other languages he speaks; by bilingual I mean a person who speaks Swahili and English, with similar qualification.

4   Interest in this possibility was stimulated by hearing a paper by David De-Camp, 'Creole language areas considered as multilingual communities', presented at the 1962 Brazzaville Conference on Multilingualism and subsequently printed in *Symposium on multilingualism* (1964). From a somewhat different standpoint, see also E. S. Klima, 'Relatedness between grammatical systems', *Language* 40:1.1–20 (1964).

5   Especially those of the 10th Meeting (February 1964), Govt. Printer (Dar-es-Salaam, 1964).

6   For a list of articles referring to the recent history of Swahili, see my 'Swahili as a *lingua franca* in East Africa', *Symposium on multilingualism* (1964).

7   For perhaps 90 percent of the population of Tanzania Swahili is taught as a second language to pupils, the majority of whom will continue to use it increasingly as their primary language, with English as the secondary language of those who go on to secondary school. There is some evidence to suggest, however, that among highly educated bilingual families in the city, some first languages, esp. Haya, Chaga, take precedence over both Swahili and English.

8   There are thus, in Bloomfield's terminology, some situations in which English is the 'upper' language, and others in which Swahili is; but in terms of interference it is Swahili which is the 'lower' language.

9   The vast majority of loans are nouns.

10 This is not easy to delimit, but if a word is used regularly in the press, on the radio, and in published words, and is accepted by a cross section of local speakers, it may be regarded as having attained general acceptance.

11 From its inception in 1930 the East African Inter-Territorial Language (Swahili) Committee has been concerned with the problem of the introduction, dissemination, and acceptance of loanwords: 'As a rule it would appear to be advisable to adopt the English terms used ... adapting the spelling so as to make it phonetic, and as far as possible fit in with the general characteristics of the Swahili' Bull. 1.2 (Dar-es-Salaam, 1930). Other views favored the adoption of Bantu words wherever possible and G. W. Broomfield argued in the same year that '... it is very much easier to Bantuize Arabic words than English words ... The majority of English words, on the other hand, are entirely foreign in structure. They are difficult for Africans to pronounce, and if they are spelt according to Swahili rules of spelling their appearance is grotesque. However, the presence of the English in the country, and the teaching of English in the schools, will make the inclusion of some English words unavoidable' ('The development of the Swahili language', *Africa* 3.516–22 [1930]). Latin and Greek, as well as other Bantu languages, were also favored as a basis for the assimilation of loans: *vokali* 'vowel'; *historia, jiografia*.

12   A good example of this is the word *wáya* 'wire'. It is said that when the Ilala
     Goods yard in Dar-es-Salaam was protected by a fence (wire), local thieves
     bemoaned their lack of booty by replying to questions *tuna waya tu* 'we've
     just got some wire!' The phrase *kuwa na waya* currently means 'to be broke'
     colloquially.

13   Main stress is indicated by (ʹ).

14   'The ideal bilingual switches from one language to the other according to
     appropriate changes in the speech situation ..., but not in an unchanged speech
     situation, and certainly not within a single sentence.' *Languages in contact* 73
     (The Hague, 1964). Compare with this, J. J. Gumperz' remark: 'Educated
     speakers tend to switch freely from one language to another when conversing
     about urban subjects, often inserting entire English phrases into their Hindi
     discourse' ('Speech variation and the study of Indian civilization', *American
     anthropologist* 63.982–3 [1961]).

15   For those unfamiliar with Bantu languages the initial *ni-* is one of a long series
     of morphemes the shape of which is determined by the noun subject, and which
     here means 'I'. The *-me-* is one of a similar series of tense-markers and here
     means 'completed action', the whole word meaning 'I have advised'.
         In a circular, the Second Vice-President has recently asked members of the
     government and others to abjure from the practice of mixing Swahili and
     English words in the manner discussed above.

16   Occasionally phrases are noted in which there is a mixture of nonloan and
     unassimilated loan, e.g. *no rinda*, 'no turn-ups', referring to a fashion in trou-
     sers.

17   As for example *mzinga* 'the beehive hairstyle for women', *mnyanyamio (mchu-
     chumio)* 'high-heeled shoes', *vitunguu*, 'woman's hairstyle in which the hair is
     gathered into small "onion-like" clusters'. There are exceptions, of course, e.g.
     stoka (der. Eng. stoker?) 'a male hairstyle in which the front hair is brushed
     up into a quiff', and *wei* (Eng. way) 'a parting' (esp. one made with a razor).

18   One of the most common at present is the phrase *pembe za chaki*, which origi-
     nally referred to the 'sidelines of the football field which are marked out in
     lime (*chaki*) and outside of which the ball is out of play'. This is now used for
     any act of behavior which is 'offside, out of court' and the defendant in a case
     is often reported as having been *kufumaniwa kwenye pembe za chaki* 'caught in
     the act', the phrase covering both the act and the place where he was caught.

19   See Leslie (1959), and his *A survey of Dar-es-Salaam* 147–8 (London, 1962).

20   Miss Joan Maw has drawn my attention also to *kozi* [kɔ́ːzi] 'course' (educa-
     tional).

21   E.g. W. H. Whiteley, 'Shape and meaning in Yao nominal classes' *ALS* 2.1–24
     (1961).

22   Noted also for nonloans by Z. S. Harris with his Comorian informant, 'In a
     given morpheme, *i* varies with ɪ as the stress shifts with change of the environ-
     ment of the morpheme' (*Structural linguistics* 114 [Chicago, 1951]).

23   'Foreign sounds in Swahili' (1946).

24   An interesting extension of this is *laifist* 'one who enjoys life', or in Swahili *mtu*

anayepiga laif. The final *-ist* may be based on the analogy, *anayepiga kinanda* 'pianist', *anayepiga taipu* 'typist'.

25 A free translation is as follows: 'When play started, both teams played equally hard, no one lagged, but Kenya Style's brilliant center-half, Mfum, defended stoutly, so that the forwards couldn't easily get through. Mfum passed cleverly to left halfback Majid, and he passed to Hemed, who passed to Kurunguja who kicked hard to Housband, and he shot immediately and that was Kenya Style one goal up. After a center when play started, Rufiji's center-half, Salamba, passes to inside-right Mikumo, and he and center-half Mfumo feinted cleverly, but Mfumo got the ball and was penalized. Mikomo took the penalty and equalized, one all.' (From *Ngurumo* July 16, 1964.)

26 See the articles by T. E. Hope 'Loan-words as cultural and lexical symbols', *Archivum linguisticum* 14:2.111–21 and 15:1.29–42 (1962–3).

13

A SYNCHRONIC AND DIACHRONIC ORDER OF RULES: MUTATIONS OF VELARS IN OLD CHURCH SLAVONIC

Valdis J. Zeps

It is a commonplace that morphophonemics to some degree mirrors history, i.e. that historical changes survive as morphophonemic alternations. Thus, the s/x alternation in Old Church Slavonic, as shown by the sigmatic aorist 1st p. sing. forms *věsъ* 'I led' and *rěxъ* 'I said' (from stems *ved* and *rek*), is a direct consequence of the historical rule 's > x || i, u, r, k ____ ' (read: s must become x in the environment after i, u, r, and k).[1]

At the same time, it is well understood that the form of cognate synchronic and diachronic rules need not agree. Thus, the synchronic form of the 'same' rule in OCS is the following: 's > x || k, g, V + ____ (+) V' (read: prevocalic morpheme-initial s must become x if preceded by a vowel or a velar).[2]

In the synchronic rule, the environment in which the change takes place has been both narrowed down (only a prevocalic morpheme-initial s changes, and no longer after an r)[3] and expanded (s changes to x after any vowel, not just i and u). The reasons for the difference in the two sets of environments are many and complex, and a few examples may be to the point here:

1. Absence of a morpheme-medial s/x change in the synchronic rule.— After an i, an s was replaced by an x as expected, e.g. **moisos* > **moixos* > *měxъ* 'flour'. A form like *běsъ* 'devil', however, which has an analogous synchronic appearance, is historically the reflex of **boidsos*, where the ds-cluster was simplified to s subsequent to the s-to-x change. There are no synchronic reasons to reconstitute the ds-cluster, and the proper synchronic treatment of the s/x opposition in *měxъ* and *běsъ* is to say that in a morpheme-medial position the s/x opposition is of lexical significance (i.e. no synchronic rule changing a medial s to x need be written).

2. Presence of the s/x change after morpheme final low vowels.—Inspection of the aorist of OCS vowel stems shows that the s/x alternation is present not only in i-stems, where it might be expected on historical grounds, e.g. *xvaliste* 'you (pl.) praised' and *xvalixъ* 'I praised', but also in a-stems, $ě$-stems, etc., e.g. *glagolaste/glagolaxъ* 'spoke', and *mъněste/mъněxъ* 'thought'. The appearance of x in *mъněxъ* and *glagolaxъ*, is thought to be due to analogy.[4]

The main argument of this paper will be the following: since cognate diachronic and synchronic rules can (or must) differ in shape, it is equally conceivable that they can (or must) differ in their order of application, i.e. the relative chronology need not agree with the descriptive order.

That such reasoning is at least plausible can be readily shown with a trivial example. The stem-final segment *d* in **ved + ti* 'to carry' is dissimilated to a spirant and assimilated in voicing to yield OCS *vesti*. In this process both synchronic and diachronic statements agree. But while there are no reasons to ever reconstruct a historical **vezti*, and the 'reasonable' diachronic progression is **vedti* > **vetti* > *vesti*, i.e. assimilation in voicing first, dissimilation in the stop-spirant feature second, in a SYN-CHRONIC grammar the devoicing rule can come very late, i.e. the progression ved + ti > vez + ti > ves + ti is perfectly acceptable.

In this paper I shall examine the so-called first and second mutations of velars in Old Church Slavonic and compare the order of statements needed for a relative chronology with that needed for a descriptive statement.

RELATIVE CHRONOLOGY. In Slavic the Indo-European (IE) inventory of velars in the environment of front vowels has been affected by three mutations—two regressive and one progressive. The so-called first (regressive) mutation changed *k*, *g*, and *x* to *č*, *ž*, and *š*, respectively, e.g. *vlъče* (voc. sing. of *vlъkъ* 'wolf'). The so-called second (regressive) mutation of velars resulted in strident dentals, e.g. *cěna* 'price' (from **kěna* < **koina*). A third set of reflexes is known as the progressive (or Baudouin de Courtenay) mutation of velars, and is illustrated by **otьkь* > *otьcь* 'father'.

While there is some disagreement as to the place of the progressive mutation (not considered here), the two regressive mutations are quite generally treated as coming in a fixed order. Crucial to the relative chronology is the intervening monophthongization of *oi* to *ě* or *i*.[5] The entire complex of changes can be schematized as follows:

1. Proto-Slavic: **vlъke*, **koina*
2. First mutation: *vlъče*, **koina*
3. Monophthongization: *vlъče*, **kěna*
4. Second mutation: *vlъče*, *cěna*.

VELAR ALTERNATIONS IN OCS. In a synchronic description of OCS morphology, we likewise have to account for both a *k/c* alternation (short for the alternation of velars with strident dentals), cognate with the second mutation, and a *k/č* alternation (short for the alternation of velars with palatals of the *č*, *ž*, *š* series), cognate with the first mutation.

In the nominal paradigm, the *k/c* alternation is encountered as follows:
(1) in the loc. sing., loc. pl., and nom. pl. of *o*-stem masculines, e.g. nom. sing. *vlъkъ*, loc. sing. *vlъcě*, nom. pl. *vlъci*, and loc. pl. *vlъcěxъ*;

(2) in the loc. sing., nom. du., and loc. pl. of *o*-stem neuters, e.g. nom. sing. *věko* 'eyelid', loc. sing. *věcě*, nom. du. *věcě*, and loc. pl. *věcěxъ*;

(3) in the dat. sing., loc. sing., and nom. du. of *a*-stems, e.g. nom. sing. *rǫka* 'hand', dat. sing. *rǫcě*, loc. sing. *rǫcě*, and nom. du. *rǫcě*

The *k/č* alternation in the nominal paradigm is restricted to the voc. sing. of the *o*-stems, e.g. voc. sing. *vlъče*.

In the pronominal declension, only two cases of alternation occur, both of the *k/c* type: nom. sing. *kъ-to* 'who', instr. sing. *cěmь*; and nom. sing. masc. *kъjь* 'which' (spelled *kyi*), nom. pl. masc. *ciji* (spelled *cii*).

The bulk of the alternations involving velars occur in the conjugation. There the *k/č* alternation is restricted to the imperative of the consonant stems, e.g. *rekǫ* 'I speak', imperative 2nd p. sing. and 3rd p. sing. *rъci*, 1st du. *rъcěvě*, 2nd du. *rъcěta*, 1st pl. *rъcěmъ*, 2nd pl. *rъcěte*. All other cases of velars before front vowels or reflexes of front vowels show the *k/č* alternation, of which we will adduce only illustrative examples:[6]

(1) before *e*: *rečemъ* 'we speak' (from rek + e + mъ);

(2) before *i*: *mǫčitъ* 'he tortures' (from mǫki + i + tъ), *kričitъ* 'he shouts' (from krikě + i + tъ), *vedeši* 'you lead' (from ved + e + xi < ved + e + si);

(3) before *a < ě*: *kričati* 'to shout' (from krikě + ti), *kričaaxъ* 'I was shouting' (from krikě + ěa + so + ъ > krič + ěa + x + ъ > krič + aa + x + ъ), *možaaxъ* (from mog + ěa + so + ъ);

(4) before *ę < ę̨*: *rěšę* 'he spoke' (from rek + s + n > rě + x + ę).

In attempting to systemize the above, we note that the morphophonemically short *e* and *ę* can be preceded only by *č*, whereas the morphophonemically long *i* and *ě* can be preceded by either a *c* (*vlъci, rǫcě, rъci, rъcěte*) or a *č* (*mǫčitъ, kričati*), i.e. *c* and *č* occur in what are substantially the same phonological environments. If, however, the immediate-constituent structure of the underlying strings is inspected, a different pattern begins to emerge for forms with *i* and *ě*:

(1) a front vowel following the velar within the same morpheme implies a *k/č* alternation, as in *mǫčitъ* (mǫki + i + tъ), *kričitъ* (krikě + i + tъ), *kričaaxъ* (krikě + ěa + so + ъ), *vedeši* (ved + e + si > ved + e + xi);

(2) in those cases where the immediate-constituent structure is obvious, a single *ě* or *i* comprising the entire morpheme implies a *k/c* alternation, as in *vlъcě, vlъci, rǫcě, rъci, rъcěte*, etc.;

(3) the *ěa* sequence of the imperfect implies a *k/č* alternation, as in *možaaxъ*;

(4) the nominal and pronominal polysyllabic terminal sequences -*ěxъ*, -*ěmь*, and -*iji* imply a *k/c* alternation.

The above listing brings some order to the distribution of the two types of alternation; nevertheless, it cannot be considered satisfactory because of the way points (3) and (4), immediately above, are formulated. Even so, a tentative rule can be formulated to account for the distribution of c as against $\check{c}$: c occurs if a velar is followed by an i or $\check{e}$ which is the sole segment of a morpheme (or is the first segment of a polysyllabic terminal sequence within the declension); otherwise, before front vowels, k alternates with $\check{c}$.

Further inspection of the terminal sequences $-\check{e}x\check{o}$, $-\check{e}m\check{o}$, and $-iji$ indicates that in the case of $-\check{e}x\check{o}$ a morpheme break is necessary to account for the appearance of an x (see introductory remarks), and that the tentative underlying string $vl\flat k + \check{e}x\check{o}$ should be replaced by $vl\flat k + \check{e} + s\check{o}$. Similarly, the morphological makeup of $ciji$ is clear—the first of the two i's comprises the nom. pl. masc. indefinite morpheme. Inspecting the form $c\check{e}m\check{o}$, with analogous considerations in mind, we discover that a morpheme boundary before $m\flat$ is implied by the whole pronominal declension. Similarly, $\check{e}$ can be detached from the stem as one of the realizations of the pronominal-oblique-theme morpheme. These considerations permit a reformulation of the rule accounting for the distribution of c and $\check{c}$: c occurs if a velar is followed by an i or $\check{e}$ which is the sole segment in a morpheme; otherwise, before front vowels, k alternates with $\check{c}$.

TERMINAL VOCALISM IN THE PRONOMINAL DECLENSION. The facts so far reviewed do not suggest that an intervening $oi > \check{e}$ change, cognate with the historical monophthongization, is necessary to account for the distribution of the k/c and $k/\check{c}$ alternations. The $oi > \check{e}$ change, however, is still very much alive in the pronominal declension, where it takes the form of an $oj/\check{e}/ej/i$ alternation. It is illustrated by the following forms of the instrumental singular: fem. $toj\varrho$ 'that', masc. $t\check{e}m\check{o}$; fem. $jej\varrho$ 'her', masc. $jim\check{o}$ 'him'; whereby oj/ej occur before vowels, $\check{e}/i$ elsewhere, and ej/i occur after palatals, $oj/\check{e}$ elsewhere. Since $c\check{e}m\check{o}$ is completely analogous to $t\check{e}m\check{o}$, an underlying $k + oi + m\flat$ must be assumed to be the starting point for morphophonemic calculations.

Since (1) an oi is needed in $koim\check{o} > c\check{e}m\check{o}$ for independent reasons, and (2) an underlying oi explains an $\check{e}/i$ ($t\check{e}x\check{o}/jix\check{o}$) alternation in the pronominal paradigm, the corpus should next be inspected with the knowledge that other instances of an $\check{e}/i$ alternation should preferably be analogous to the $t\check{e}x\check{o}/jix\check{o}$ alternation.

$\check{e}/i$ ALTERNATION. We have already seen that the type of alternation where an i occurs after a palatal and an $\check{e}$ elsewhere can best be explained by an underlying oi/ei alternation (see above). The same alternation takes place in the nominal declension, where loc. sing. $vl\flat c\check{e}$ ($vl\flat k + oi$) apparently has the same morphological structure as loc. sing. $kon\frown i$ 'horse' ($kon\frown +$ $oi > kon\frown + ei$), dat. and loc. sing. $r\varrho c\check{e}$ ($r\varrho k + oi$) the same structure as loc. sing. *duši* 'soul' (duš + oi > duš + ei), etc. In the conjugation, however, the *ě/i* alternation in the imperative, as in *rьci/rьcěte*, does not fit the pattern of '*i* after a palatal, *ě* elsewhere', and there can be no advantage in treating the *i* of *rьci* as a synchronic reflex of *oi*. There may be some merit to analyzing *rьcěte* as rьk + oi + te, but only if there are reasons for treating forms of the type *sěji/sějite* 'sow' as fully analogous to *rьci/rьcěte* rather than to *moli/molite* 'pray'. There are certainly no reasons for reconstituting an *oi* in the nom. pl. of nouns such as *vlьci*.

ORDER OF RULES. Now that the reasons for the *ě/i* alternation have been considered, we are ready to give a new version of the underlying forms for illustrative words considered, and to write a set of rules explaining them. The forms are as follows: loc. sing. vlьk + oi, nom. pl. vlьk + i, loc. pl. vlьk + oi + sъ, loc. sing. věk + oi, loc. pl. věk + oi + sъ, dat. sing. rǫk + oi, voc. sing. vlьk + e, instr. sing. k + oi + mь, nom. sing. masc. k + i + j + i, 2nd p. sing. imperat. rьk + i, 2nd p. pl. imperat. rьk + ě + te or rьk + oi + te, 1st p. pl. pres. rek + e + mъ, 3rd p. sing. pres. mǫki + i + tъ, krikě + i + tъ, 2nd p. sing. pres. ved + e + si, and 1st p. sing. imperf. mog + ěa + so + ъ.

The following ordered rules account for the phonetic realization of these underlying strings:

1. s > x ‖ k, g, V + _____ (+) V: vlьk + oi + xъ, věk + oi + xъ, ved + e + xi, mog + ěa + xo + ъ;
2. oi > ě: vlьk + ě, vlьk + ě + xъ, věk + ě, věk + ě + xъ, rǫk + ě, k + ě + mь, rьk + ě + te;
3. k, g, x > c, dz, s ‖ _____ + i, ě +: *vlьcě, vlьcěxъ, vlьci, věcě, věcěxъ, rǫcě, cěmь, ciji, rьci, rьcěte*;
4. k, g, x > č, ž, š ‖ _____ + FV: *vlьče*, mǫči + i + tъ, kričě + i + tъ, *vedeši*, mož + ěa + xo + ъ;
5. V > zero ‖ _____ + V: *mǫčitъ, kričitъ*, mož + ěa + x + ъ;
6. ě > a ‖ č, š, ž, j + _____: *mǫžaaxъ*.

REASONABLE ALTERNATIVES. There are a number of reasonable alternatives to the proposed synchronic order of *oi > ě, k > c*, and *k > č*. Most of the alternatives involve the assumption of a different base form for a number of strings; let us consider one such set of assumptions.

a. Let us assume that the nom. pl. masc. and imperat. sing. morphemes of the shape *i* are (synchronically) reflexes of a back diphthong, say, *ъi̯*.

b. Let us further assume that nominal forms are assembled according to the formula 'stem + stem vowel + (pronominal oblique theme) + case ending' and are subject to a vowel-dropping rule, as are the verbal forms.

If both of the above proposals are adopted, underlying strings such as vlьk + o + oi + xъ and rьk + ъi can be constructed for *vlьcěxъ* and *rьci* as against, say, rek + e + tъ and krikě + i + tъ for *rečetъ* and *kričitъ*. Then the order of the rules can parallel the historical order, and the following sequence can be proposed:

1. k > č ‖ ____ (+)FV: *rečetъ*, kričě + i + tъ;
2. V > zero ‖ ____ + V; ъi > i and oi > ě: vlьk + ě + xъ, rьk+ i, *kričitъ*;
3. k > c ‖ ____ (+)FV: *rьci*, *vlьcěxъ*.

The major disadvantage of the alternative just proposed is that it divides into two parts what apparently is one rule, i.e. the rule that determines where a *k* alternates with a *c* and where with a *č*. Such a rule should, probably, be formed by consolidating rules (3) and (4) of 'Order of rules' above, as follows:

$$\text{k, g, x} > \begin{cases} \text{c, dz, s} \ \| \ \_\_\_\_ + \begin{Bmatrix} \text{i} \\ \text{ě} \end{Bmatrix} + \\ \text{č, ž, š} \ \| \ \_\_\_\_ (+)\text{FV} \end{cases}$$

There are strong intuitive reasons for agreeing with the above formulation, in that the unified rule considers the special cases first (i.e. first eliminates *k*, *g*, *x* from the less general environment '____ + i, ě, +' where *k*, *g*, *x* change to *c*, *dz*, *s*), and only then prescribes the more general *k*, *g*, *x* > *č*, *ž*, *š* change.

DISCUSSION. There are a number of methodological implications to the proposition that the synchronic and diachronic orders need not agree.

First, it suggests a renewed examination of the set of assumptions that is used as a matter of routine in historical reconstruction, but is not explicitly stated. Involved in this case is the automatic, perhaps perfectly justified, assumption that there is some sort of priority to the formula 'velars before front vowels' [k, g, x ‖ ____ (+)FV], which must be kept constant and other statements varied to maintain this constancy. The above assumption, in turn, is a direct consequence of a more general one that morpheme boundaries cannot be used as an environmental factor in sound change, i.e. that the environment '____ + i, ě +' does not constitute a proper environment for a velar mutation.

The strong possibility that the synchronic and diachronic order of rules can disagree, furthermore, casts doubt on the credibility of internal reconstruction, especially if it involves the type of detail and time depth encountered in reconstructions of Proto-IE from IE, and the like.

At the same time, the rise of formal grammar has reoriented historical linguistics in a way that is as unexpected as it is exciting. In addition to discussing the history of individual sounds and individual morphemes, or even the history of phonological systems and paradigmatic sets, linguists can now anticipate the writing of histories of grammars. These grammars will include, of course, the comparison of cognate rules in their historical and synchronic shapes; of such comparison the present paper is a modest instance.

NOTES

1   The following symbols have been employed in this paper: two vertical lines ($\|$) separate the process side of the rule on the left from the environment side on the right, an underlined blank space (____) indicates where the process takes place, a plus sign denotes a morpheme boundary, parentheses encompass optional elements, V stands for any vowel, FV stands for any front vowel, and braces ({ }) surround parallel but ordered branches of one and the same rule.
2   So formulated in my 'Optional rules in the formation of the Old Church Slavonic aorist', *Language* 60.35 n. 6c (1964).
3   It is not clear to me whether OCS *mrěxъ* 'I died' is synchronically derived from mer + so + ъ via mrě + so + ъ or via mer + xo + ъ. In the latter case, *r* would be part of the synchronic environment as well.
4   As suggested in Paul Diels, *Altkirchenslavische Grammatik* §114 Anm. 1 (Heidelberg, 1932).
5   The double reflex of *oi* as *ě* and *i* under apparently identical phonological conditions (cf. Diels §11 Anm. 2) is one of the main reasons why the synchronic and diachronic versions of the velar mutation rules cannot be equated.
6   Omitted are those cases where *č* < *kj*; the *kj* > *č* replacement is illustrated by assemblies and replacements of the type plaka + e + tъ > plakj + e + tъ > *plačetъ* 'he cries', and is not directly relevant to this paper.

INDEX

'analytic': vs. 'synthetic' views, 4

analytic grammar: linguistic interest in design of, 63; pedagogical need for Sanskrit, 63; objectives and uses of, 63–4; components of, 64–5; methodological procedures for, 64; operations to be accounted for, 65; order of operations, 65–8; resolution of unanalyzed residue, 68–9; lists and rules of, 69–72; with reference to IC analysis, 107; vs. transformational grammar, 111

Andrews, S., Jr.: cited, 7

approximation theory: relationship to topology, 36; extended to 'continuity' and language theory, 37; relationship to translation problems, 37

Arabic: verbal base forms in, 27–31

Bailey, N.: dictionary by, 78

Bantu: Zaramo, 126; loans, 139

base form: need for lexicon and derivation of verbal system, 27; information required of, 28; inadequacies of traditional, for Arabic, 28; advantages of specially constructed forms for Arabic, 28–31

Bazell, C. E.: cited, 92, 98–9, 100, 101, 104

binary cuts: in IC analysis, 91; questioning of, 104

Blinkenberg, A.: comments on work of, 115, 117

Bloch, B.: cited, 93, 94; comments on work of, 100, 108

Bloomfield, L.: comments on work of, 89, 100

breath group: as minimal unit of French verbal syntax, 118

Cantor, G.: comments on work of, 34

Cauchy, A. L.: comments on work of, 34

causal chains: leading to recognition of universals, 47

causality theory, 47

Chatman, S.: cited, 100; comments on work of, 106

Chinese. *See* Mandarin Chinese

cognate rules: disagreement of synchronic and diachronic, 145, 146; orders of application of, 146

computer(s): contribution of, 5; relationship to mechanical translation, 5; relationship to simplicity criterion, 5; for automatic parsing programs, 106–7

conditioners: tabulation of, 50–8; class of, 58–9; phonetic-phonemic state of, 59; applications of descriptive data of, 59

constituent(s): in Sanskrit grammars, 63; in IC analysis, 91

constitute(s): in Sanskrit grammars, 63; in segmentation procedures, 90; meaning of, 90

construction: in IC analysis, 90–1

constructional grammar, 103

constructional homonymy: provision for, 97

'continuity': historical introduction of concept to mathematics, 34; generalization of concept to topology, 34; tentative definition of, 35; and invariance as dual concepts, 35; as a type concept, 36; lessons derived from new definition of, 36; formal definitions of, 39

contrastive grammar: emphasis on practical applications, 81; for clarification of linguistic structures, 81

controversies: in the history of linguistic science, 3

Cowan, G. M.: mentioned, 42